¡Listos!

Rachel Aucott

2 Verde

Teacher's Guide

heinemann.co.uk

✓ Free online support
✓ Useful weblinks
✓ 24-hour online ordering

01865 888058

Inspiring generations

Heinemann Educational Publishers,
Halley Court, Jordan Hill, Oxford OX2 8EJ.

Part of Harcourt Education Limited.

Heinemann is the registered trademark of
Harcourt Education Limited.

© Rachel Aucott

First published 2003

07 06 05 04
10 9 8 7 6 5 4 3 2

A catalogue record is available for this book from the
British Library on request.

ISBN 0 435 42963 9

Produced by Ken Vail Graphic Design.

Original illustrations © Heinemann Educational Publishers 2003

Cover photograph by Eye Ubiquitous/Paul Thompson

Printed in the UK by Athenaeum Press Ltd

Tel: 01865 888058 www.heinemann.co.uk

Contents

Introduction

¡Listos! is a lively and easy-to-use Spanish course for pupils aged 11–16 of a wide ability range, which supports Foundation Subjects MFL, including the Framework for teaching MFL. The materials are fully differentiated with parallel Pupil's Books from stage 2.

Teaching Foundation Subjects MFL and the MFL Framework using *¡Listos!*

Framework objectives

¡Listos! ensures that there is comprehensive coverage of all five strands of the framework:

✓ **Words** – teaching pupils to practise the meaning, spelling and sound of Spanish words together.
✓ **Sentences** – teaching pupils how to write simple grammatically correct sentences.
✓ **Texts: reading and writing** – teaching pupils how to understand and write more complex text using connectives, pronouns and verbs.
✓ **Listening and speaking** – linking listening and speaking to help pupils speak more accurately and authentically.
✓ **Cultural knowledge and contact** – giving pupils the opportunity to learn about Spain and other Spanish-speaking countries.

All the **framework objectives** for Year 7 are **launched** and **reinforced** in *¡Listos! 1*. The reinforcement of an objective often takes place in a number of units.

Details of where the objectives are launched and reinforced are given:

a) in the Framework Overview grid on pages 12–13 of this Teacher's Guide to help you with your **long-term planning;**
b) in the Teacher's Guide in the overview grids at the beginning of each module (e.g. page 14) to help you with your **medium-term planning:**
c) in the Teacher's Guide in the overview boxes at the start of each teaching unit to help with your **short-term (i.e. lesson) planning.**

In addition, all activities in the Pupil's Book are cross-referenced to the MFL Framework to allow you to launch or reinforce the teaching objectives at different points in the course if you wish. The references are given in the Teacher's Guide at the start of each activity.

Lesson starters

Every unit in the Pupil's Book contains two lesson starters: the first at the beginning of every unit, the second approximately halfway through the unit at the point when a second lesson is likely to begin. All of the starters are described in the Teacher's Guide. Most of them are simple ideas that allow you to recap on previous knowledge or prepare the pupils for new language to be learnt in the unit. They are designed to get the lesson off to a brisk start, focusing the pupils' attention and promoting engagement and challenge. Some of the activities have an accompanying copymaster in the Resource and Assessment File. These copymasters include worksheets, games cards and material which can be photocopied onto overhead transparencies.

Plenaries

Every unit in the Pupil's Book ends with a plenary session. Again, these are simple ideas described in the Teacher's Guide. They aim to draw out the key learning points. Pupils are actively involved and are expected to demonstrate and explain what they have learnt in the unit. They identify links with what the pupils have learnt so far and what they will learn later in the course.

Thinking skills

Thinking skills are integrated into many of the starters as well as into some of the Pupil's Book activities themselves. Many of the Skills sheets in the Resource and Assessment File also involve thinking skills.

The components

¡Listos! 2 verde consists of:
Pupil's Book
Cassettes/CDs
Workbooks
Resource and Assessment File
Teacher's Guide
Flashcards
Colour OHT File

Pupil's Book

The Pupil's Book consists of six theme-based modules which are subdivided into six or seven double-page units. The last unit (*¡Extra!*) is an extension unit and can be left out if you are short of time or if it is not suitable for your pupils. It contains activities in all four skill areas and is to be used with whole classes in the same way as the other units. The activities tend to be slightly more difficult than in the core units, with longer reading and listening passages, which bring together the language of the module. No new core language is introduced.

¡Extra! is followed by two pages of module word lists (*Palabras*) organised by topic to help with vocabulary learning and revision.

At the end of each module there is a checklist of key functions and structures (*Resumen*) and revision activities that can be used as a practice test (*Prepárate*).

At the back of the Pupil's Book there are three sections of further practice and reference. The *Te toca a ti* section contains self-access differentiated reading and writing activities. *Te toca a ti A* is for lower-ability and *Te toca a ti B* for higher-ability pupils. There is a grammar reference and practice section where all the grammar points introduced in the core units are explained fully and accompanied by practice activities. Finally, there is a comprehensive Spanish–English word list, a shorter English–Spanish word list and a list of instructions covered in the Pupil's Book.

Cassettes/CDs

There are three cassettes/CDs for *¡Listos! 2 verde*. These contain listening material for both presentation and practice. The material includes dialogues, interviews and songs recorded by native speakers. The listening material for all the *Pruebas* (the formal assessment tests in the Resource and Assessment File) can be found on the final CD/cassette.

Workbook

For *¡Listos! 2 verde* there is an accompanying workbook (Workbook A). This provides self-access reading and writing tasks which are designed to be fun. The workbook is ideal for homework. There is a page of activities for each double-page core unit in the Pupil's Book. There are also one or two pages of revision material (*¡Extra!*), one or two pages of grammar practice and a self-assessment page at the end of each module (*Resumen*).

Resource and Assessment File

The Resource and Assessment File is organised into modules for ease of use and contains the following photocopiable material.

1   Worksheets/OHT masters to support starter activities.

2   Sheets consisting of pictures with the matching Spanish words/phrases on a corresponding sheet.

3   Grammar worksheets (*Gramática*) for more practice of grammar points introduced in the Pupil's Book. The Teacher's Guide gives guidance on where these sheets fit into the scheme of work. They can clearly be used at any later point in the scheme.

4   Skills sheets, practising language learning skills (e.g. dictionary work) introduced in the Pupil's Book. Many involve thinking skills.

5   Module word lists (*Vocabulario*): photocopiable versions of the word lists from the Pupil's Book.

6   *Resumen*. A pupil checklist of language covered.

And for assessment:

1   *Pruebas*: end-of-module (and end-of-year) tests for formal assessment, together with the teaching notes and the answers for the tests.

2   Target-setting sheet for pupils and pupil-friendly descriptors of the NC Attainment Target Levels.

Teacher's Guide

The Teacher's Guide contains:

● overview grids for each module
● clear teaching notes and full recording transcript
● suggestions for starters and plenaries
● mapping of activities to the Framework, the National Curriculum and 5–14 Guidelines
● guidance on using the materials with pupils of varying abilities
● suggestions for additional differentiated practice
● suggestions for ICT activities
● suggestions for numeracy and literacy activities
● help with using Spanish in the classroom

Flashcards

There are 48 full-colour, single-sided flashcards with the name of the object in Spanish on the reverse for presentation or practice of language. A complete list of flashcards is given on page 7.

OHT File

There are 16 full-colour transparencies and 16 overlays for presentation or practice of language. The file contains detailed teaching notes on how and where in the course to use the OHTs.

Using *¡Listos! 2 verde* with pupils of different ability

After initial teacher-led presentation work with the whole class, pupils move on to a range of individual, pair and group activities, which allow them to work at different levels. There is a lot of scope in the core material for differentiation by pace and outcome. Suggestions are provided in the Teacher's Guide. The last unit (*¡Extra!*) is an optional extension unit. The activities in the Pupil's Book are supplemented by those in the *Te toca a ti* section at the back of the book. For each module there is a double page of activities: the A page activities are at reinforcement level and the B page activities are at extension level. For ease of use these activities are clearly flagged in the Teacher's Guide. Further differentiation is provided by means of the two parallel workbooks.

For those pupils who are ready to focus on the underlying structure of the language the grammar boxes in the teaching units are backed up by full explanations and practice in the grammar section at the back of the Pupil's Book as well as in the grammar worksheets. These activities can be done at any appropriate point. Although these tasks might be more suitable for higher-ability learners, it is assumed that most pupils will be able to attempt at least some of them during the year.

Introduction

Grammar

The key structures being used in a unit are often presented in a grid on the Pupil's Book page, providing support for speaking and writing activities. A summary of the key structures of each whole module is given in the *Resumen* at the end of each module. Key grammar points are highlighted in *Gramática* boxes on the page and there is a reference and practice section at the back of the Pupil's Book. In addition, there are worksheets which specifically focus on grammar in the Resource and Assessment File.

Progression

There is a clear progression within each module of the Pupil's Book and language is systematically revised and extended throughout the book. Clear objectives are given in the Teacher's Guide at the beginning of each unit to help teachers plan the programme of work which is appropriate for different ability groups.

Assessment for Learning

Revision and self-assessment

¡Listos! 2 verde encourages learners to revise and check their own progress regularly. At the end of each module there is a *Resumen*, a checklist of key language covered. There is also a version of the *Resumen* in the workbooks, in the form of a page of open-ended writing.

Some starters and plenaries encourage pupils to reflect on their performance and how to improve it. In addition, the target-setting sheet in the Resource and Assessment File Framework Edition allows pupils to record their NC level in each Attainment Target and set themselves improvement targets for the next module. The File also contains the NC level descriptors in pupil-friendly language, to help with their target-setting.

Teacher assessment

The assessment scheme consists of ongoing assessment as well as more formal periodic assessment. The scheme in *¡Listos! 2 verde* focuses on Levels 1–5 in the four National Curriculum Attainment Targets (Levels C to E for the 5–14 Guidelines).

All activities have been matched against National Curriculum levels and the 5–14 Guidelines to assist teachers in carrying out continuous assessment. It must be stressed that performance in an individual activity can only contribute towards evidence that a pupil is achieving that level. Pupils must successfully carry out a range of activities at a particular level in order for the level to be awarded.

The end-of-module (and end-of-year) tests or *Pruebas* in the Resource and Assessment File provide a more formal means of assessment. The *Prepárate* in the Pupil's Book provides activities that will help pupils to prepare for the tests. The tests cover all four skills and can be used with pupils of all abilities. Again, the tasks are matched against NC levels.

The teaching sequence

Lesson starter (see page 4)

Presentation

New language can be presented using the cassettes or CDs, ensuring that pupils have authentic pronunciation models. However, the range of resources in the scheme enables the teacher to vary the way new language is presented.

Flashcards: These can be used in a variety of ways. Ideas for using the flashcards are included in the teaching notes. A list of the flashcards is given on page 7.

Visuals or picture sheets: The Resource and Assessment File contains picture sheets for each module. These can be photocopied and cut up for games or copied onto an overhead transparency and used for presentation work.

Colour overhead transparencies: These can be used for presentation or revision. The Colour OHT File contains detailed teaching notes with suggestions for additional practice.

Practice

Pupils move on to a variety of activities in which they practise the new language, usually in pairs or groups. Many of the practice activities are open-ended, allowing them to work at their own pace and level.

Reinforcement and extension

The units often end with a more extended activity of an open-ended nature. Pupils of all abilities can work on the same basic task and the teacher has an opportunity to work with individuals or small groups.

To cope with the range of ability in a class, additional reinforcement and extension activities are provided in the Pupil's Book (*Te toca a ti*) as well as the differentiated workbooks, already described.

Plenary (see page 4)

Using the target language

Instructions in the first two modules of the Pupil's Book are in Spanish and English. Thereafter they are translated into English the first time they appear. They have been kept as simple and as uniform as possible.

Integrating ICT

Suggestions for ICT activities have been included in the Teacher's Guide. These activities use the following types of software which are likely to be already available in schools.

Word-processing software

The essential difference between word processing

and writing with pen and paper is that a word-processed text need never be a final product. Since errors can be corrected and texts can be developed and improved without spoiling the appearance of the work, writers gain the confidence to experiment as well as the motivation to take a more active interest in the language they are using.

Graphics software

Graphics software could take the form of word-processing programs that can import images, desktop publishing programs or graphics programs.

Learners can use this software to produce posters, booklets and leaflets in which they display newly acquired language in an attractive and original way. They can experiment with layout and select from a range of type styles and sizes as well as graphics.

Each module of *¡Listos! 2 verde* contains suggestions for ICT activities.

There are also links to relevant websites in this book. In order to ensure that they are up to date, that the links work and that the sites are not inadvertently linked to sites that could be considered offensive, we have made them available on the Heinemann website at www.heinemann.co.uk/hotlinks
When you access the site, the express code is 9639T.

Games

Card games

The word/picture sheets in the Resource and Assessment File can be used for:

1 Matching pictures and labels.

2 Matching pictures and labels: Set a time limit and see which pair finishes first.

3 Pelmanism or pairs: A series of pairs of cards are laid face down in random order. Pupils match the pictures with the labels. The winner is the person who manages to make the most pairs.

4 Guessing: Each pupil has four or more cards positioned so they can see the cards but their partner can't. Pupils take it in turns to guess their partner's cards using the structures and vocabulary from the unit. First one to guess all correctly is the winner.

Vocabulary games

1 Pupils make own cards to play Pelmanism (drawing pictures and writing their own labels from the unit).

2 Spelling bees: Do these at the end of each unit.

3 Noughts and crosses (in a pair or whole-class team-game played on the board): Almost all

vocabulary and structures linked to a unit can be practised playing this game.

Practising vocabulary: as in the Pupil's Book. The vocabulary being introduced is numbered. You/ pupils write these numbers on a grid. Pupils guess what the word is for each number to get a nought or a cross (with or without looking in the Pupil's Book, depending on how difficult you want to make it).

4 Wordsearches: These are used throughout the book; however as an extension activity you could ask pupils to make up their own wordsearches.

5 'I went to market and I bought …': Each pupil repeats the previous word and adds their own. This can be adapted for different topics.

6 Cracking codes: Get pupils to write their own code for partners to crack. Use the symbol function on a computer to make up a code.

7 Telephones: Write a variety of made-up telephone numbers on pieces of paper (keep a list of these numbers). Hand out to pupils. The first pupil reads out a number and carries out a conversation with the person whose number it is, e.g. *¡Hola! ¿Cómo te llamas?* etc. Keep the pace fast. To make it more difficult pupils could ask how the name is spelt and write it down.

Number games

Once pupils have learnt numbers 1–20 there are lots of number games for them to practise.

1 Mexican wave: Pupils stand up as they say their number and then sit down.

2 Lotto/bingo:
   a quick lotto (use as a lesson starter): Ask pupils to choose seven numbers from, for example, 1 to 20. Pupils tick off their numbers as they are called out. First one to tick all numbers shouts out 'lotto'.
   b bingo: Same as lotto, except pupils draw a grid of, for example, 12 boxes and write the numbers in the boxes.

3 Buzz: Pupils all stand up and count from, for example, 1 to 20, and leave out multiples of, for example, five. Instead of saying this they must say 'buzz' or 'vaya'. If they forget and say the multiple of five they are out and must sit down.

4 Counting with a soft toy: Count round the class throwing a soft toy.

5 Rub out the number on the board: Divide the board in half. Write the same numbers but in a different place on each half of the board. One member from each team stands in front of the board with chalk or a boardmarker and tries to be the first to cross out the number called out. Keep a tally showing which team has scored the most points.

Answers to *Gramática* activities (Pupil's Book pages 120–132)

1 Nouns (p.121)

1 regalos
2 cartas
3 invitaciones
4 lugares
5 viajes
6 edades
7 peces

4.1 Cardinal numbers (p.122)

1	99	**d**	noventa y nueve
2	107	**e**	ciento siete
3	111	**g**	ciento once
4	120	**h**	ciento veinte
5	550	**b**	quinientos cincuenta
6	1999	**c**	mil novecientos noventa y nueve
7	2002	**a**	dos mil dos
8	2003	**f**	dos mil tres

5 Dates (p.123)

Pupil's own responses.

6.4 Talking about frequency

Pupil's own responses.

7. Agreement of adjectives (p.124)

1 Tengo los ojos   **d** marrones
2 Mi gato es   **c** blanco y negro
3 Las paredes de mi dormitorio son   **b** amarillas
4 La alfombra es   **a** blanca

7.1 Comparatives (p.124)

Pupil's own opinions.

7.2 Superlatives (p.125)

Pupil's own details.

12 Questions (p.127)

Examples:

1 ¿Cómo te llamas?
2 ¿Dónde vives?
3 ¿Qué tipo de comida te gusta?
4 ¿Cuándo es tu cumpleaños?
5 ¿Cuál es tu nombre? (¿Cuáles son tus pasatiempos favoritos?)
6 ¿Cuánto es? (¿Cuántos años tienes?/¿Cuántas zapatillas tienes?)
7 ¿Quién es?(¿Quiénes son?)
8 ¿Por qué te gustan las películas románticas?

¿Quieres salir conmigo esta noche?
¿Te hacen falta toallas?
¿Hablas español?

List of flashcards

1 los huevos
2 las verduras
3 la carne
4 la sopa
5 un helado
6 el pescado
7 el pollo
8 los perritos calientes
9 las chuletas
10 el flan
11 las gambas
12 los plátanos
13 las peras
14 las uvas
15 las lechugas
16 las cebollas
17 las aceitunas
18 una botella de limonada
19 200 gramos de queso
20 500 gramos de jamón
21 una barra de pan
22 un cartón de leche
23 un paquete de galletas
24 una caja de pasteles
25 una lata de sardinas
26 un parque temático
27 un espectáculo de flamenco
28 un campo de golf
29 una fiesta de caballos
30 una pista de tenis
31 descansar
32 nadar en el mar
33 tomar el sol
34 ir de paseo
35 ir a discotecas
36 montar en bicicleta
37 sacar fotos
38 hacer surfing
39 el club de jóvenes
40 el parque de atracciones
41 la bolera
42 la pista de hielo
43 tener fiebre
44 tener insolación
45 tener tos
46 tener diarrea
47 tener una picadura
48 tener catarro

Covering the Programmes of Study

The table below indicates where in ¡Listos! 2 verde pupils have the opportunity to develop the skills and understanding prescribed in the National Curriculum Programmes of Study. For each area we have indicated where these appear in the core units of the Pupil's Book. There are further opportunities both in the Pupil's Book and the supplementary components. More detail is provided in the grids at the beginning of each module in this Teacher's Guide. Some skills are more appropriate or are practised more easily at later stages of language learning. Where this is the case we have indicated at what stage of ¡Listos! pupils will encounter these.

1 Acquiring knowledge and understanding of the target language – pupils should be taught:	
a the principles and relationships of sounds and writing in the target language	2.3; 3.6; 5.2; 6.3
b the grammar of the target language and how to apply it	Throughout
c how to express themselves using a range of vocabulary and structures	Throughout

2 Developing language skills – pupils should be taught:	
a how to listen carefully for gist and detail	1.5,7; 2.1,2; 3.3,4; 4.2,3; 5.1,3; 6.2,3
b correct pronunciation and intonation	2.3; 5.2; 6.3
c how to ask and answer questions	1.1,4; 2.2,3,5; 4.2; 5.1,2,4,5 6.3
d how to initiate and develop conversations	1.3; 4.2; 5.1,4;5
e how to vary the target language to suit context, audience and purpose	1.6,7; 2.6; 4.1; 5.3,4
f how to adapt language they already know for different contexts	1.1,4; 2.1,5; 4.1
g strategies for dealing with the unpredictable	
h techniques for skimming and for scanning written texts for information, including those from ICT-based sources	2.6,7; 4.6; 5.6
i how to summarise and report the main points of spoken or written texts, using notes where appropriate	1.4; 1.7; 2.1,2; 5.2; 6.3
j how to redraft their writing to improve its accuracy and presentation, including the use of ICT	1.3,6 4.4

3 Developing language-learning skills – pupils should be taught:	
a techniques for memorising words, phrases and short extracts	3.6; 5.2
b how to use context and other clues to interpret meaning	3.7; 5.3
c to use their knowledge of English or another language when learning the target language	1.6; 3.6
d how to use dictionaries and other reference materials appropriately and effectively	1.6; 2.2, 3.1; 4.1;3,6;
e how to develop their independence in learning and using the target language	Throughout

4 Developing cultural awareness – pupils should be taught about different countries and cultures by:	
a working with authentic materials in the target language, including some from ICT-based sources	1.7; 2.5,6; 3.1,7; 5.2,3; 6.6
b communicating with native speakers	1.6,7; 2.1; 4.3; 5.4
c considering their own culture and comparing it with the cultures of the countries and communities where the target language is spoken	1.3; 2.1,2,5,7; 3.5; 4.1,6; 5.4
d considering the experiences and perspectives of people in these countries and communities	1.7; 2.7; 3.5; 5.3; 4.6; 5.4; 6.5

5 Breadth of study – during key stages 3 and 4, pupils should be taught the knowledge, skills and understanding through:	
a communicating in the target language in pairs and groups, and with their teacher	Throughout
b using everyday classroom events as an opportunity for spontaneous speech	Throughout
c expressing and discussing personal feelings and opinions	2.2; 3.2,3,5; 5.2
d producing and responding to different types of spoken and written language, including texts produced using ICT	1.7; 2.7; 3.7; 4.3,6; 6.4
e how to use a range of resources, including ICT, for accessing and communicating information	1.2,3,6; 2.1,2,3,5,6; 3.4,5; 4.1,2,3,4; 5.2,4,5; 6.3,4,5
f using the target language creatively and imaginatively	1.7; 2.6; 4.1; 5.3
g listening, reading or viewing for personal interest and enjoyment, as well as for information	2.7; 6.1
h using the target language for real purposes	2.1,6; 4.1; 5.3
i working in a variety of contexts, including everyday activities, personal and social life, the world around us, the world of work and the international world	Throughout

Note: 2.1 = Module 2, Unit 1

¡Listos! 2 for Scotland (verde)

All the activities in the *¡Listos! 2* Pupil's Book are matched to the 5–14 Guidelines. The following table shows where the different Strands feature in *¡Listos! 2 verde*. The table does not list every occurrence of a strand. It is designed to illustrate the range of coverage in the course. There are additional opportunities throughout the course which are clearly marked in this Teacher's Guide.

Information regarding the level(s) of an activity is given in the teaching notes in this Guide.

Strand	Module 1	Module 2	Module 3	Module 4	Module 5	Module 6
Listening for information and instructions	Unit 2, ex. 1	Unit 5, ex. 1c	Unit 3, ex. 3a	Unit 4, ex. 2	Unit 2, ex. 1a	Unit 3, ex. 3b
Listening and reacting to others*						
Listening for enjoyment		Unit 7		Unit 6		Unit 1, ex. 2a
Speaking to convey information	Unit 5, ex. 4	Unit 3, ex. 2b	Unit 4, ex. 2			Unit 5, ex. 1c
Speaking and interacting with others	Unit 4, ex. 3b	Unit 3, ex. 2b	Unit 1, ex. 2b	Unit 2, ex. 2	Unit 4, ex. 3	Unit 2, ex. 1b
Speaking about experiences, feelings and opinions	Unit 6, ex. 1b	Unit 1, ex. 1b	Unit 7, ex. 2	Unit 4, ex. 3a	Unit 2, ex. 2b	Unit 6, ex. 3
Reading for information and instructions	Unit 1, ex. 1a	Unit 4, ex. 2a	Unit 2, ex. 1a	Unit 6, ex. 1	Unit 3, ex. 1	Unit 5, ex. 4a
Reading aloud						
Reading for enjoyment						
Writing to exchange information and ideas	Unit 5, ex. 6	Unit 2, ex. 3c	Unit 6, ex. 2b	Unit 5, ex. 4	Unit 1, ex. 4	Unit 4, ex. 3c
Writing to establish and maintain personal contact	Unit 6, ex. 1c	Unit 1, ex. 3b		Unit 3, ex. 2b	Unit 4, ex. 5	
Writing imaginatively/to entertain	Unit 3, ex. 3	Unit 6, ex. 4b	Unit 3, ex. 3c	Unit 1, ex. 2c	Unit 5, ex. 3	Unit 3, ex. 2b

* Since this strand is so closely linked to 'Speaking and interacting with others' it is not listed separately.

Coverage of the MFL Framework Objectives in ¡Listos! 1 and 2

The following charts show coverage of the Framework Objectives in ¡Listos! 1 and 2.

The charts indicate where an objective is launched and reinforced. The reinforcement of an objective often takes place in a number of units and the reference here is just an example.

Year 7 Objectives

Objective	Launch	Reinforcement	Objective	Launch	Reinforcement	Objective	Launch	Reinforcement	Objective	Launch	Reinforcement	Objective	Launch	Reinforcement
7W1	1.1	4.4	7S1	1.8	5.3	7T1	2.6	5.3	7L1	1.1	4.5	7C1	2.7	5.5
7W2	1.5	5.2	7S2	1.5	6.3	7T2	1.6	4.2	7L2	2.3	5.3	7C2	3.7	5.7
7W3	1.2	1.7	7S3	1.3	2.5	7T3	2.6	4.6	7L3	2.3	3.1	7C3	3.3	5.5
7W4	1.2	2.1	7S4	1.1	2.3	7T4	3.3	4.6	7L4	2.1	6.4	7C4	2.4	5.5
7W5	1.3 (present) 4.3 (preterite)	5.1	7S5	1.2	1.8	7T5	2.6	3.5	7L5	3.6	4.3	7C5	1.1	5.3
7W6	1.6	3.5	7S6	3.1	5.5	7T6	3.3	3.4	7L6	1.5	4.6			
7W7	4.3	5.2	7S7	3.4 (present) 5.6 (preterite) 6.5 (imm. future)	3.7	7T7	3.2	5.6						
7W8	1.4	5.7	7S8	1.2	2.3									
			7S9	1.6	5.1									

References are to ¡Listos! 1
1.2 = Módulo 1, Unit 2

Coverage of the MFL Framework Objectives

Year 8 Objectives

Objective	Launch	Reinforcement	Objective	Launch	Reinforcement	Objective	Launch	Reinforcement	Objective	Launch	Reinforcement	Objective	Launch	Reinforcement
8W1	2.1r 2.2v	5.2	8S1	3.1	4.3r 6.4v	8T1	2.5r 4.1v	6.4r 4.3v	8L1	1.4r 2.4v	2.5r 3.3v	8C1	*	*
8W2	2.1r 2.2v	5.2	8S2	3.6r 3.5v	5S.r 4.3v	8T2	4.3r 4.4v	4.5r 5.4v	8L2	6.4	6.6	8C2	1.1	1 Te toca a ti
8W3	*	*	8S3	4.1r 3.6v	6.5r 6.3v	8T3	1.6	5.7r 2.7v	8L3	1.5r 2.3v	4.2	8C3	1.7	3.5
8W4	1.1	3.2r 1.3v	8S4	1.1	6.6r 5.1v	8T4	1.6	4.7r 2.1v	8L4	2.2	5.2r 4.4v	8C4	6.1r 2.7v	6.1v
8W5	1.2r 2.5r 4.3r 1.5v 3.4v 4.4v	2.6r 3.4r 4.4r 2.6v 3.6v 4.5v	8S5	1.4	2.6	8T5	5.6r 4.1v	6.2r 4.3v	8L5	5.2	*	8C5	2.5	5.4 5.1v
8W6	4s		8S6	1.1	5.2r 6.2v	8T6	1.6	4.3r 3.5v	8L6	5.1	5.4			
8W7	2.7r 3.7v	4.7r 4.6v	8S7	1.1r 3.4r 4.3r 1.1v 3.4v 4.4v	4.5r 5.5v	8T7	all	all						
8W8	3.6r 4.1v	6.4	8S8	3.6r 4.6v	4.1r 6.6v									

References are to *¡Listos! 2*
r = *rojo*
v = *verde*
References without r or v apply to both books.
S = Skills Sheet

Year 9 Objectives

Objective	Launch	Reinforcement	Objective	Launch	Reinforcement	Objective	Launch	Reinforcement	Objective	Launch	Reinforcement	Objective	Launch	Reinforcement
9W1	5.2		9S1	*		9T1	1.7	All 'Extra' 2.7	9L1	3.3r	5.1r	9C1	*	*
9W2	5.6r	5.7r	9S2	3.6r	'Extra' 3.7r	9T2	1.7	4.3r	9L2	3.4r	6.6r	9C2	1 Te toca a ti	
9W3	*		9S3	4.3r	4.7r	9T3	1.7	All 'Extra'	9L3	4.7r	5.4r	9C3	3.7	5.2
9W4	3.4r	4.4r	9S4	5.4	6.6r	9T4	All 'Extra' 1.6	All 'Extra' 6.1r	9L4	2.7r	6.6r	9C4	2 Te toca a ti r 4.6v	4.1r
9W5	1.7	4.5r	9S5	*	*	9T5	5.3	6.6r	9L5	5.2r		9C5	4.1	5.4
9W6	1.2r		9S6	5.6r	5.7r	9T6	6.5r		9L6	6.1r 6.3v	6.3r			
9W7	4s		9S7	5.6r	6.6r	9T7	Through-out	Through-out						
9W8	All 'Extra' 1.7	All 'Extra' 2.7	9S8	4.7r										

References are to *¡Listos! 2*
r= *rojo*
v= *verde*
References without r or v apply to both books.
'*Extra*' = Extension spreads at end of each Módulo.
Prep. = *Prepárate* (practice test)
Te toca a ti = self-access reading and writing section

13

Unit	Key Framework objectives	PoS	Key language and Grammar
1 Son muy famosos (pp. 6–7) Talking about yourself: Giving your name Saying how old you are Giving your nationality Saying where you live Describing yourself Talking about other people: Asking what their name is Asking how old they are Asking where they come from Asking what they look like	8W4 Word endings [L] 8S4 Question types [L] 8S7 *Present, past, future* [L] 8S6 Substituting and adding [L] 8C2 Famous people [L]	2c ask and answer questions 2f adapt language for different contexts	*Tener: tengo, tienes, tiene* *Ser: soy, eres, es* *Vivir: vivo, vives, vive* *¿Cómo te llamas? Me llamo …* *¿Cuántos años tienes? Tengo … años.* *¿Cuál es tu nacionalidad? Soy …* *¿Dónde vives? Vivo en …* *¿Tienes hermanos? Sí, tengo un hermano/una hermana.* *No, no tengo hermanos. Soy hijo único/ Soy hija única.* *¿De qué color son tus ojos? Tengo los ojos azules.* *¿Cómo es tu pelo? Tengo el pelo rubio/ondulado.* *¿Eres alto o bajo? Soy alto/Soy bajo.* *¿Eres alta o baja? Soy alta/Soy baja.*
2 Soy el más inteligente de la clase (pp. 8–9) Making comparisons	8W4 Word endings [R]	5e range of resources	Comparatives: *más + adjective + que* Superlatives: *el/la más + adjectives* Agreement of adjectives with nouns *Clara es más alta que Verónica.* *Iván es más bajo que Diego.* *Mario es el más generoso de la clase.* *Guapo/a* *Inteligente* *Divertido/a* *Simpático/a*
3 Mucho gusto (pp. 10–11) Introducing yourself Introducing friends and family	8W4 Word endings [R]	2d initiate/ develop conversations 2j redrafting writing 4c compare cultures 5e range of resources	Demonstrative pronouns: *éste, ésta, éstos, éstas* *Te presento a mi familia.* *Ésta es mi madre.* *Éste es mi padre.* *Éstas son mis primas.* *Éstos son mis tíos.* *Se llama(n) …* *Encantado(a).* *Mucho gusto.* *¿Qué tal el viaje?*
4 Estás en tu casa (pp. 12–13) Asking for what you need Saying what you need Saying that you are missing something	8S5 Negative forms and words [L]	2c ask and answer questions 2i report main points 2f adapt language for different contexts	Pronouns: *me, te, le + hace(n) + falta* *¿Necesitas una toalla?* *Sí, necesito una toalla/No, no necesito una toalla.* *¿Te hace(n) falta champú/pasta de dientes?* *Sí me hace(n) falta … /No, no me hace(n) falta …*
5 Unos regalos (pp. 14–15) Buying gifts for someone Describing someone's personality	8W4 Word endings [R] 8W5 Verbs (present) [L]	2a listen for gist and detail	Indirect object pronouns: *me, te, le, le* *¿Qué compras para tu abuelo?* *Le compro una gorra.* *Es hablador/a.*

Unit	Key Framework objectives	PoS	Key language and Grammar
6 Muchas gracias por el regalo (pp. 16–17) Writing a thank-you letter Choosing an introduction Giving your thanks Saying what you like/don't like about the present Choosing an ending	8T3 Language and text types [L] 8T4 Dictionary use [L] 8T6 Text as model and source [L]	2e adapt language 2j redraft writing 3c use knowledge of English 3d use reference materials 4b communicating with native speakers 5e range of resources	*Querido(a)(os)(as) … /¡Hola!* *amigo(a)(os)(as)/familia/abuelo(a)(os)(as)* *Muchas gracias por el regalo.* *Es (muy)(bastante) interesante/fantástico(a).* *Me encanta/Me gusta.* *No me gusta.* *Lo/la detesto.* *Eres simpático(a).* *Sois simpáticos(as).* *Escríbeme pronto/Hasta pronto/Recuerdos a todos/* *No me escribas nunca más.* *Saludos/besos/abrazos/adiós.*
Resumen y Prepárate (pp. 18–19) Pupil's checklist and practice test	8S6 Substituting and adding [R]		
¡Extra! ¡Escríbeme Pronto! (pp. 20–21) Optional unit: Teenage magazine (Mega Pop)	9W5 Verbs (conditional) [L] 9T1 Understanding complex language [L]	2a listen for gist and detail 2e adapt language 2i report main points 4a working with authentic materials 4b communicating with native speakers 4d consider experiences in other countries 5d different text types 5f using the TL creatively	*Mándanos* *Cartear* *Envíanos* *Aficionado* *Mantener correspondencia con …* *Las motos* *Los peluches* *Un extraterrestre* *Un ser humano* *Abiertas* *Salir por ahí*
Te toca a ti (pp. 108–109) Self-access reading and writing at two levels	8C2 Famous people [R] 8S4 Question types [R]		

1 Son muy famosos

(Pupil's Book pages 6–7)

Main topics

- Talking about yourself:
  Giving your name
  Saying how old you are
  Giving your nationality
  Saying where you live
  Describing yourself

- Talking about other people:
  Asking them what their name is
  Asking how old they are
  Asking where they come from
  Asking what they look like

Key Framework objectives

- Word endings 8W4 (Launch)
- Question types 8S4 (Launch)
- Present, past, future 8S7 (Launch)
- Substituting and adding 8S6 (Launch)
- Famous people 8C2 (Launch)

Grammar

- Tener: tengo, tienes, tiene
- Ser: soy, eres, es
- Vivir: vivo, vives, vive

Key language

¿Cómo te llamas? Me llamo …
¿Cuántos años tienes? Tengo … años.
¿Cuál es tu nacionalidad? Soy …
¿Dónde vives? Vivo en …
¿Tienes hermanos? Sí, tengo un hermano/una hermana.
No, no tengo hermanos. Soy hijo único/ Soy hija única.

¿De qué color son tus ojos? Tengo los ojos …

azules	negros
verdes	grises
marrones	

¿Cómo es tu pelo? Tengo el pelo …

rubio	largo
castaño	rapado
negro	liso
pelirrojo	rizado
corto	ondulado

¿Eres alto o bajo? Soy alto/Soy bajo.
¿Eres alta o baja? Soy alta/Soy baja.

Resources

Cassette A, side 1
CD 1, track 2
Cuaderno, page 3

Starter 1: [8S4]

Aim: To revise the three personal questions *¿Cómo te llamas? ¿Cuántos años tienes? ¿Dónde vives?*; intonation with questions.

Use a bean bag, fluffy toy, or a ball. Ask pupils to stand or form a circle. Throw the ball to a pupil and ask the first question. They must answer and throw the ball back. Continue with the other two questions and then go back to the beginning. As you go round the class speed up the pace. If a pupil drops the ball, he/she must sit down. Encourage correct intonation.

Suggestion

Quickly revise basic descriptions from *¡Listos! 1*. You could use OHTs 11 and 12 (also from book 1) and ask a couple of volunteers to describe the facial features. Or, stick two posters of a couple of celebrities on the board. Ask pupils to work in pairs and then describe their facial features. You might also want to re-introduce your puppets and have a few conversations with some of the pupils in the class asking them their names, how old they are, what they look like. You could get a couple of pupils to ask the puppets some questions (keep it humorous!).

1a Lee la información sobre Enrique y Jennifer. Empareja las preguntas con las respuestas. (AT3/3) [8S4,7; 8C2]

✉ *Reading for information/instructions, Level C*

Reading. Pupils look at the identity cards for Enrique Iglesias and Jennifer López on page 6. Ask them to match the questions (numbered) with the answers (lettered).

Answers

Enrique Iglesias:	1 e	2 d	3 a	4 b	5 c
Jennifer López:	1 b	2 a	3 e	4 c	5 d

1b Escucha y comprueba tus respuestas. (AT1/2)

Listening. Pupils listen to the recording and check their answers. You could suggest that pupils swap books and mark their partner's answers.

Tapescript

¿Cómo te llamas?
Me llamo Enrique Iglesias.
¿Cuántos años tienes?
Tengo 28 años.
¿Cuál es tu nacionalidad?

Soy español.
¿Dónde vives?
Vivo en Miami.
¿Tienes hermanos?
Sí, tengo un hermano y una hermana. Mi hermana se llama Chabelí y mi hermano se llama Julio.

¿Cómo te llamas?
Me llamo Jennifer López.
¿Cuándo es tu cumpleaños?
Mi cumpleaños es el 24 de julio.
¿De qué color son tus ojos?
Tengo los ojos marrones.
¿Cómo es tu pelo?
Tengo el pelo largo, ondulado y castaño.
¿Eres alta o baja?
No soy ni alta ni baja. Soy mediana.

1c Con tu compañero/a, haz entrevistas con Enrique y Jennifer. (AT2/3) [8S4]

✉ *Speaking and interacting with others, Level C/D*

Speaking. Working in pairs, pupils take it in turns to interview their partner who takes the role of Enrique or Jennifer.

1d Con tu compañero/a, haz y contesta a las preguntas de **1a**. (AT2/3) [8W4; 8S4]

✉ *Speaking and interacting with others, Level C/D*

Speaking. Working in pairs, ask pupils to use the vocabulary frame on page 7. To help them ask two confident pupils to ask and answer one question from **1a** as an example.

➕ Drama. Pupils should sit in a circle. You could start off by asking the pupil on your left the first question in the vocabulary frame. They answer and then ask the person on their left the next question and so on until you complete the frame. Then go back to the beginning. To help everyone concentrate (and make it a little bit more difficult!) introduce a rhythmic clapping before starting the questions: clap hands, clap knees, click fingers.

Starter 2: [8S4]

Aim: To revise 'question' words and their spelling.

Brainstorm. Without looking in their books, ask pupils to give you as many question words as they can think of. Write these on the board. Keep the pace fast. e.g. *¿Cómo?, ¿Cuántos?, ¿Cuál?, ¿Dónde?* Point out that many question words have an accent. Now ask them to think up common questions to go with these. If there is time, go round the class and ask pupils the questions.

Alternatively, supply possible endings for pupils to match with the question words e.g. *¿… te llamas?, ¿… años tienes?, ¿… es tu nacionalidad?, ¿… vives?*

2a Lee la información de **1a** otra vez y escribe E (Enrique) o J (Jennifer). (AT3/3) [8C2]

✉ *Reading for information/instructions, Level C*

Reading. Pupils look at the identity cards again and then answer questions 1–7 on page 7 by writing E or J for the above next to numbers 1–7. Suggestion: set a time limit and see who completes the questions first.

Answers

| 1 J | 2 E | 3 E | 4 E | 5 J | 6 E | 7 J |

2b Escribe cuatro frases similares sobre un/a amigo/a. (AT4/2–4) [8W4; 8S6,7]

✉ *Exchange information/ideas, Level C/D*

Writing. Pupils use the verbs in the *Gramática* box to help them write four sentences to describe a friend.

2c Escribe frases similares sobre otra persona famosa. (AT4/2–4) [8W4]

✉ *Exchange information/ideas, Level C/D*

Writing. Ask pupils to use the same verbs they have just used in **2c** to write similar sentences about a celebrity.

🖙 **ICT activity**

Pupils use a desktop/wordprocessing package to make up an interview with someone famous. They could draw or insert a picture of that person as well.

En casa.

Personal dossier. This was introduced in *¡Listos! 1* and is intended to be an ongoing project throughout the book. Pupils compile information about themselves using what they have learnt. Here you could ask them to make up an identity card for themselves and one for someone they admire.

Plenary

To recap questions covered in this unit. Ask pupils to imagine they have to interview someone famous. They should list the four most important questions they would ask.

Cuaderno A, page 3

1a Elige tres dibujos para cada descripción. (AT3/3)

✉ *Reading for information/instructions, Level D*

Reading. Pupils choose three symbols, letters a–f, to illustrate the two descriptions (Francisco and Clara).

Answers

Francisco: b, d, e
Clara: a, c, f

1b Lee las descripciones de **1a** otra vez y contesta a las preguntas. (AT3/3)

✉ *Reading for information/instructions, Level D*

Reading. Pupils read the descriptions in activity **1a** again and write down Francisco's name or Clara's name to answer questions 1–5.

1 Francisco	**2** Francisco	**3** Francisco
4 Clara	**5** Francisco	

1c Escribe una descripción similar sobre ti. (AT4/2–4) [8T6]

✉ *Exchange information/ideas, Level C/D*

Writing. Pupils use the two letters to help them write a description about themselves.

2 Soy el más inteligente de la clase

(Pupil's Book pages 8–9)

Main topics

Making comparisons

Key Framework objectives

● Word endings 8W4 (Reinforcement)

Grammar

● Comparatives: *más* + adjective + *que*
● Superlatives: *el/la más* + adjectives
● Agreement of adjectives with nouns

Key language

Clara es más alta que Verónica.
Iván es más bajo que Diego.
Mario es el más generoso de la clase.
Guapo/a
Inteligente
Divertido/a
Simpático/a

Resources

Cassette A, side 1
CD 1, tracks 3 and 4
Cuaderno A, page 4
OHTs 1 and 2

Starter 1: [8W4]

Aim: To revise adjective agreement. Glossary practice.

Display on the board or have an OHT prepared of the following adjectives:
alto, alta, grande, pequeño, pequeña, bajo, baja, antiguo, antigua, inteligente

Ask your pupils to: **1** Write down the meaning of each adjective. They should look words up in the glossary if they are unsure of the meaning; **2** Write down why you have written two of each adjective on the board. What is the difference (*o* and *a* endings)? What do these differences mean (agreement of adjectives with masculine nouns and feminine nouns)? **3** Which adjectives are the odd ones out (*grande, inteligente*)? See if someone can point out that these remain the same for both masculine and feminine nouns.

1 Escucha y lee. Empareja cada frase con el dibujo apropiado. (AT1/2) [8L3]

✉ *Listening for information and instructions, Level B*

Listening. Pupils listen to the recording and match sentences 1–5 with the appropriate picture a–e.

Answers

1 c	**2** d	**3** a	**4** e	**5** b

Tapescript

1 *Clara es más alta que Verónica.*
2 *Blanca y Gloria son más pequeñas que Chulo y Arnold.*
3 *Iván es más bajo que Diego.*
4 *Roma es más antigua que Milton Keynes.*
5 *Dúgal es más grande que Pepe.*

2 Con tu compañero/a, describe a las personas de la foto. ¿Verdad (✓) o mentira (✗)? (AT2/3) [8W4]

✉ *Speaking and interacting with others, Level C*

Speaking. Working in pairs, pupils use the *Gramática* grid to help them compare the people in the photo on page 8.

Starter 2: [8W4]

Aim: To recap comparatives.

Ask different pupils to stand up and volunteers from the rest of the class to compare their heights. Alternatively, draw stick pictures on the board and ask pupils to write their comparisons down. Take feedback.

3a Elige la frase apropiada para cada dibujo. (AT3/2) [8W4]

✉ *Reading for information/instructions, Level C*

Reading. Pupils match sentences a–e at the top of page 9 with the appropriate drawings 1–5.

Answers

a 5	**b** 3	**c** 1	**d** 2	**e** 4

3b Escucha y comprueba tus respuestas. (AT1/2)

Listening. Pupils listen to the recording and correct their answers.

Tapescript

1 *Emma es la más alta de la clase.*
2 *Teresa es la más baja.*
3 *El señor Reyes es el profesor más divertido del instituto.*
4 *Mario es el más generoso de la clase.*
5 *Sara es la más inteligente de los estudiantes.*

3c Escribe frases similares sobre tus compañeros/as de clase. (AT4/3) [8W4]

✉ *Exchange information/ideas, Level B/C*

Writing. Pupils use activity **3a** and the *Gramática* box on Superlatives to help them compose a few sentences about their class mates.

4 Lee la carta de Gerardo. ¿Verdad (✓) o mentira (✗)? (AT3/4) [7T1]

✉ *Reading for information/instructions, Level D*

Reading. Ask pupils to read Gerardo's letter to Oscar. They then answer questions 1–6 with *verdad* (✓) or *mentira* (✗).

Suggestion: Remind pupils to use the glossary to help them with any vocabulary they are stuck on.

Answers

1 ✗ 2 ✓ 3 ✗ 4 ✗ 5 ✓ 6 ✗

☞ **ICT activity**

Wordprocessing. Provide a template letter with gaps in appropriate places either similar to the letter on page 9 or replicated. Type in the missing vocabulary at the bottom of the page. Ask pupils to fill in the gaps by 'inserting' or 'moving' the appropriate words from the bottom of the page.

En casa.

Personal dossier. Ask pupils to use the comparatives and superlatives they have just met to help them write down a few thoughts about school (friends, school subjects, teachers etc.).

Plenary

Ask pupils to write down two things to explain the differences between comparatives and superlatives. Then ask one or two volunteers to come up and explain their thoughts to the rest of the class. Does everyone agree with them?

Cuaderno A, page 4

1a Empareja los dibujos con las frases. (AT3/2) [8W4]

✉ *Reading for information/instructions, Level C*

Reading. Pupils match pictures a–e with sentences 1–5.

Answers

1 b 2 c 3 a 4 e 5 d

1b Lee las frases de **1a** otra vez y escribe sus nombres. (AT3/2) [8W4]

✉ *Reading for information/instructions, Level C*

Reading. Pupils read the sentences in activity **1a** again and write down the the names for each of the characters in pictures a–e.

Answers

a Hugo (bigger), Pepi **b** Javier, Alejandro (taller) **c** Rafael (quieter), Miguel **d** Daniel (more fun), Mauricio **e** Bernardina, Saturnina (shorter)

2a Lee la carta. ¿Verdad (✓) o mentira (✗)? (AT3/4)

✉ *Reading for information/instructions, Level D*

Reading. Pupils read the letter and answer questions 1–6 with a tick (verdad) or a cross (mentira).

Answers

1 ✓ 2 ✗ 3 ✓ 4 ✗ 5 ✗ 6 ✓

2b Lee la carta otra vez y contesta a las preguntas. (AT3/4)

✉ *Reading for information/instructions, Level D*

Reading. Pupils read the letter again and answer questions 1–4.

Answers

1 La Paz (Bolivia) 2 (language) student 3 English and French 4 a tallest b most handsome c youngest

Main topics

- Introducing yourself
- Introducing your family and friends

Key Framework objectives

- Word endings 8W4 (Reinforcement)

Grammar

- Demonstrative pronouns: *éste, ésta, éstos, éstas*

Key language

Te presento a mi familia.
Ésta/Éste es mi …

madre   *padre*
hermano/a   *tío/a*
abuelo/a   *primo/a*
Éstas/Éstos son mis tías/tíos.
Se llama(n) …
Encantado(a).
Mucho gusto.
¿Qué tal el viaje?

Resources

Cassette A, side 1
CD 1, tracks 5 and 6
Cuaderno A, page 5
Grammar Resource and Assessment file, page 7
OHTs 3 and 4

Starter 1 [8W4]

Aim: Revision of family members.

Write the first letter only of each family member on the board. Ask pupils to fill in the gaps. Working in pairs, see who can complete this gap filling exercise the fastest. The winning pair must also tell you who each member is in English. Can anyone explain the clues provided by '*a*' and '*o*' endings?

Example. m _ _ _ _ , p _ _ _ _ , h _ _ _ _ o, h _ _ _ _ _ _ , p _ _ _ a, etc.

Suggestion

Use OHTs 3 and 4 to help introduce family members.

1a Lee y escucha [8W4; 8S4]

✉ *Reading for information/instructions, Level D*

Reading/Listening. Ask pupils to follow the introductions at the top of page 10 and listen to the recording.

Tapescript

– *Te presento a mi familia. Ésta es mi madre, Claudia.*
– *Hola, Oscar. ¿Qué tal el viaje?*
– *Muy bien, gracias.*
– *Éste es mi padre, Ignacio.*
– *Hola, Oscar.*
– *Encantado.*
– *Ésta es mi hermana, Lucía.*
– *Mucho gusto.*
– *Ésta es mi abuela, doña Mercedes.*
– *Hola, Oscar. ¡Bienvenido!*
– *Éstos son mis tíos y mi primo. Mi tío se llama Jorge. Mi tía se llama Ana María. Y mi primo se llama Héctor.*
– *Éstas son mis primas. Se llaman Pilar, Paloma y Esme.*

1b Eres Gerardo. Empareja los nombres con las palabras apropiadas. (AT3/3) [8W4]

✉ *Reading for information/instructions, Level D*

Reading. Ask pupils to choose the word that corresponds to each name. Get them to copy the grid at the bottom of page 10 and fill it in with the appropriate family member.

Answers

Doña Mercedes (mi abuela), Lucía (mi hermana), Ana María (mi tía), Jorge (mi tío), Héctor (mi primo), Pilar (mi prima)

1c Copia y completa las frases sobre Gerardo. (AT3/3) [8W4]

✉ *Reading for information/instructions, Level D*

Writing. Ask pupils to fill in the blanks with members of Gerardo's family.

Answers

1 madre   **2** Ignacio   **3** hermana   **4** abuela   **5** Ana María
6 primas

Starter 2 [8W4]

Aim: To recap family members and demonstrative adjectives.

Ask pupils to bring in photos of their family, friends or pets and talk about them to their partner. e.g. *Éste es mi perro Pepe, éste es mi ratón Paco y ésta es mi hermana Camila.*

2a Mira los dibujos y empareja las frases. (AT3/3) [8W4]

✉ *Reading for information/instructions, Level C*

Reading. Pupils use the drawings **a** and **b** to help them match sentences 1–8 with sentences a–h.

Answers

| 1 d | 2 g | 3 a | 4 h | 5 c | 6 e | 7 f | 8 b |

2b Escucha y comprueba tus respuestas. (AT1/2)

Listening. Pupils listen to the recording and check their answers.

Tapescript

1 *Éste es mi abuelo. Se llama Carlos.*
2 *Éste es mi padre. Se llama Luis.*
3 *Éste es mi hámster. Se llama Savi.*
4 *Éste es mi ratón. Se llama Figo.*
5 *Éstos son mis tíos. Mi tío se llama Juan y mi tía se llama Nieves.*
6 *Éste es mi gato. Se llama Trufa.*
7 *Éste es mi hermano. Se llama Martín.*
8 *Ésta es mi prima. Se llama Susana.*

ICT activity

Fun with texts. Enter simple vocabulary, for example, family members in 1–8 or some of the sentences (once they have been matched up) in activity **2a**. Jumble these up using 'enigma'. Ask pupils to work in pairs, or threes and unscramble the words. Listen to the recording to correct.

2c Con tu compañero/a, elige un dibujo 'a' o 'b' y presenta a las personas. (AT2/3–4) [8W4]

Speaking and interacting with others, Level C/D

Speaking. Ask pupils to choose one of the drawings **a** or **b** and introduce the characters to their partner.

3 Escribe frases similares sobre una familia famosa. (AT4/3) [8W4]

Writing imaginatively, Level C/D

Writing. Ask pupils to write sentences to introduce a famous family.

➕ Get them to swap papers with a partner to see if they can guess who the famous family is.

ICT activity

Wordprocessing. Type up exercise **3**. The advantage of this is that mistakes can be easily corrected and work can be presented without the discouragement of numerous 'red pen' marks – Pupils can then file away a nicely presented piece of work!

En casa.

Personal dossier. Ask pupils to stick a photo in their dossier or draw a picture of family members or favourite pets and introduce them by writing a phrase on each.

Plenary

Ask pupils to work with a partner and write down how to say 'this' and 'these' in Spanish. Why are there four ways to say 'this' and 'these' in Spanish?

Cuaderno A, page 5

1a Mira el árbol genealógico y completa las frases con las palabras del cuadro. No necesitas todas las palabras. (AT3/3)

✖ *Reading for information/instructions, Level C*

Reading. Pupils use the family tree and words in the box to complete sentences 1–10 to show the relationship of the people with each other. Not all the words in the box will be needed. Point out to pupils that if they are stuck they can use the direct article at the beginning of each sentence to give them a clue. For example '*el*' tells you that the person needed is male, '*la*' the person will be female, '*los*' there will be two people (not necessarily both male: one could be male and the other could be female.)

Answers

| 1 tío | 2 hermana | 3 abuelo | 4 tía | 5 prima | 6 hermano |
| 7 madre | 8 tíos | 9 abuela | 10 padres |

1b Dibuja el árbol genealógico de tu familia y describe qué relación tienes con cada persona. (AT4/2)

✖ *Writing to exchange information/ideas, Level B*

Writing. Pupils draw their own family tree and write down the name and who each person is in relation to themselves.

Grammar, Resource and Assessment File, page 7

Some key verbs

1

Pupils fill in a grid with 1st person singular, 3rd person singular and 3rd person plural verb forms in the present tense.

	Tener	Ser	Vivir
	To have	To be	To live
I	tengo	soy	vivo
He	tiene	es	vive
She	tiene	es	vive
They	tienen	son	viven

2

Making comparisons

Pupil's look at the artwork prompts and make appropriate sentences using the comparatives *más* and *menos*.

Answers

a Juan es más alto que Pedro.
b Ana es más pequeña que Conchi.
c Neli es más grande que Lala.
d Miguel es más joven que Chus.
e Isabel es más inteligente que María.

3

Demonstrative adjectives

Pupils choose the correct demonstrative adjective to complete each sentence.

Answers

a Éste es mi tío.
b Ésta es mi amiga Begoña.
c Éstos son mis animales.
d Éstos son mis padres.
e Ésta es mi hermana mayor.
f Éste es mi abuelo.

4 Estás en tu casa

(Pupil's Book pages 12–13)

Main topics

- Asking for what you need
- Saying what you need

Key Framework objectives

- Negative forms and words 8S5 (Launch)

Grammar

- Pronouns: *me, te, le,* + *hace(n)* + *falta*

Key language

¿Necesitas una toalla?
Sí necesito una toalla/No, no necesito una toalla.
¿Te hace(n) falta …?
champú   *gel de ducha*

pasta de dientes   *jabón*
un cepillo de dientes   *desodorante*
gel de baño   *colonia*

Sí, me hace falta champú/No, no me hace falta champú.

Resources

Cassette A, side 1
CD 1, tracks 7, 8 and 9
Cuaderno A, page 6
Starter 2, Resource and Assessment File, page 4
Hojas de trabajo, Resource and Assessment File, pages 5 and 6 (*colonia, un cepillo de dientes, pasta de dientes, una toalla, champú, gel de ducha, jabón, desodorante*)
OHTs 5 and 6

Starter 1: [8S5]

Aim: Revision of pronouns + *gustar/encantar*; applying high frequency words across topic areas.
Me/Te gusta(n)/No me gusta(n)
Me/Te encanta(n)/No, no me encanta(n)

Write the following four things on the board: *jugar al fútbol, el chocolate, los ratones, las sandalias.* Add more if you wish. Check that pupils remember when to use *gusta, encanta* and when to use *gustan, encantan.*

Ask pupils to write down whether they like/love or dislike the above.

Pupils now ask their partner whether they like/love or dislike the above:
¿Te gustan las sandalias? No, no me gustan las sandalias. You may wish to model a question and answer with your class first.

Suggestion

Bring in a selection of the items at the top of page 12. Pull them out of a shopping bag and say what they are, getting your class to repeat the items with you. Play the memory game: placing the items on a table, cover them with a cloth. Ask pupils to close their eyes and remove one item. When they open their eyes ask *¿Me hace falta(n) …?* See if anyone can guess correctly. Remember: no peeking!

1 Escribe el orden en que se mencionan las cosas. (1–8) (AT1/1)

✉ *Listening for information and instructions, Level A*

Listening. Ask pupils to write down the letter of the picture in the order in which they are mentioned on the recording.

Answers

1 f	2 a	3 g	4 e	5 b	6 h	7 d	8 c

Tapescript

1 un cepillo de dientes
2 una toalla
3 colonia
4 pasta de dientes
5 desodorante
6 gel de baño o de ducha
7 jabón
8 champú

☞ ICT activity

Text salad (*Fun with texts*). To practise, load the vocabulary from activity 1. Use 'enigma' to jumble up the words which pupils unscramble without help, or use 'copywrite easy' that reveals the initial letters only so that pupils fill in the blanks.

2 Escucha. Copia y rellena el cuadro. (AT1/3) [8S5; 8L3]

✉ *Listening for information and instructions, Level D*

Listening. Pupils copy the writing grid on page 12, listen to the recording and fill in the grid with the things that are missing (*le hace falta*) and not missing (*no le hace falta*).

Answers

Le hace falta: h (gel de baño), a (una toalla), e (pasta de dientes).
No le hace falta: d (jabón), c (champú), g (colonia), b (desodorante) f (cepillo de dientes)

Tapescript

– Aquí está tu dormitorio .Y aquí está el cuarto de baño. ¿Te hace falta gel de ducha o jabón?
– Sí, me hace falta gel de ducha. No necesito jabón.
– El gel está aquí. ¿Necesitas algo más? ¿Una toalla, o champú?
– Necesito una toalla.
– Toma, una toalla. ¿Te hace falta colonia o desodorante?
– No gracias, pero me hace falta pasta de dientes.
– Toma, pasta de dientes. ¿Te hace falta un cepillo de dientes?
– No gracias, tengo un cepillo de dientes.

Starter 2 [8S1]

Aim: To recap pronouns + *hacer falta*; word order.

Using *Resource and Assessment File*, page 4 give each pupil a card with a word on. Ask pupils to arrange themselves in groups of three or four in the correct order. (e.g. *me/hace falta/un/libro*) If something like *hace falta un libro me* appeared, this would be wrong. Quickly check that everyone has made a sensible sentence. For an extra challenge you could give each group enough cards for two sentences.

3a Mira la foto en 1. ¿Qué necesitan estas personas? (1–5) (AT1/3) [8L3]

Listening for information and instructions, Level D

Listening. Pupils look at the photo in activity **1** and listen to the recording. They write down the items needed in 1–5.

Answers

1 d	2 h	3 a	4 c	5 b, e

Tapescript

1 – ¿Te hace falta una toalla?
  – No, gracias, tengo una toalla pero necesito jabón.
  – Toma, jabón.
  – Gracias.
2 – ¿Necesitas algo?
  – Me hace falta gel de ducha.
  – El gel de ducha está aquí en la estantería.
3 – Necesito una toalla, por favor.
  – Las toallas están en el armario.
  – Gracias.
4 – ¿Te hace falta champú?
  – Sí, sí, necesito champú.
  – Hay champú en el cuarto de baño.
  – Vale.
5 – ¿Necesitas algo?
  – Pues, me hacen falta el desodorante y la pasta de dientes.
  – Toma, desodorante. Y la pasta de dientes está aquí.
  – Muchas gracias.

3b Con tu compañero/a, pregunta y contesta. (AT2/3) [8S5]

Speaking and interacting with others, Level C

Speaking. Working in pairs, pupils ask their partner what they need or don't need.

Game.

Working in pairs, ask pupils to draw three things or write down three things on a folded piece of paper. Each takes it in turn to guess what their partner needs. e.g.¿*Te hace falta pasta de dientes? Sí, me hace falta/No, no me hace falta.* The person to guess all three things first is the winner.

4 Empareja los dibujos con las frases. (AT3/2) [8W5]

Reading for information/instructions, Level C

Reading. Pupils match sentences 1–6 with drawings a–f.

Answers

1 e	2 a	3 b	4 f	5 d	6 c

5 ¿Qué te hace falta para ir de vacaciones? Escribe una lista. (AT4/2–3)

Exchange information/ideas, Level A/B

Writing. Ask pupils to write a list of the things they need when they go on holidays.

ICT activity

Use an artwork package such as 'paintbox'. Ask pupils to do a series of humorous pictures and label them.

Use *Fun with texts*. Load in the language from each speech bubble (a–f). Use 'prediction' or 'copywrite easy' to re-write the speech bubbles.

Plenary

Quick fire questions round the room. How do you say 'I need' 'you need' 'he needs' 'she needs' 'I need toothpaste' 'you need towels', etc.

Cuaderno A, page 6

1 ¿Qué le hace falta comprar a Esperanza? Mira lo que hay en la cesta y marca lo que hay en la lista. (AT3/1)

Reading for information/instructions, Level A

Reading. Pupils look at the basket and tick what is on the list.

Ask pupils to write down in English the items from the list that still need to be bought.

Answers

> Pasta de dientes, un cepillo de dientes, gel de ducha, jabón

2 Mira los dibujos y completa los globos usando las palabras en el cuadro. (AT3/2, 4/2) [8W5]

✉ *Exchange information/ideas, Level B*

Reading/Writing. Pupils look at drawings 1–6 and complete the speech bubbles with suitable words from the writing grid.

Answers

> **1** ¿Necesitas gel de ducha?/¿Te hace falta gel de ducha?
> **2** ¿Te hace falta un cepillo de dientes?/¿Necesitas un cepillo de dientes?
> **3** Me hace falta una toalla./Necesito una toalla.
> **4** Me hace falta jabón./Necesito jabón.
> **5** ¿Necesitas colonia?/¿Te hace falta colonia?
> **6** Me hace falta pasta de dientes./Necesito pasta de dientes.

Hojas de trabajo, Resource and Assessment File, pages 5 and 6

Cards for pairwork featuring items of toiletry and gifts: pupils match the pictures to the correct words.

5 Unos regalos
(Pupil's Book pages 14–15)

Main topics
- Buying gifts for someone
- Describing someone's personality

Key Framework objectives
- Word endings 8W4 (Reinforcement)
- Verb tenses (present) 8W5 (Launch)

Grammar
- Indirect object pronouns: *me, te, le, le*

Key language
¿Qué compras para tu …
madre   padre
abuelo/a   hermano/a

Le compro …
una gorra   una lata de galletas
una camiseta   un CD
una caja de chocolates

Es …
hablador/a   simpático/a
tranquilo/a   deportista
serio/a   sociable

Resources
Cassette A, side 1
CD 1, tracks 10, 11 and 12
Hojas de trabajo, Resource and Assessment File, pages 5 and 6 (*una camiseta, una gorra*)
Cuaderno A, page 7

Starter 1 [8W5]

Aim: To practise the endings to regular *–ar* verbs. 1–3 person singular.

Write on the board, *yo habl…/ tú habl…/ él habl…/ ella habl…*

Ask pupils to write the ending to each on mini whiteboards or a piece of paper. Do this one at a time and ask pupils to hold their boards up, checking that each person has written the correct ending.

Now write another. e.g. *comprar*. See if anyone can tell you what it means. Ask pupils to write down in Spanish 'I buy', 'you buy', 'he buys'. First you may need to break this down a little bit. e.g. Ask what endings would you need to add if you remove *–ar* from *comprar* to say 'I buy', etc.

1 Empareja los regalos con las personas. (AT1/3) [8L3]

✕ *Listening for information and instructions, Level D*

Listening. Pupils listen to the recording and match the people 1–5 with the presents a–e.

Answers

1 c   2 b   3 e   4 d   5 a

Tapescript

– *Voy a comprar regalos para la familia de Gerardo.*
– *¿Qué compras para la abuela de Gerardo?*
– *Le compro bombones.*
– *¿Qué compras para la hermana de Gerardo?*
– *Le compro una camiseta de Londres.*
– *¿Qué compras para el padre de Gerardo?*
– *Le compro un CD.*
– *¿Y para la madre de Gerardo?*

– *Le compro una caja grande de galletas.*
– *Y ¿qué compras para Gerardo?*
– *Le compro una gorra del Manchester United.*

2 Con tu compañero/a, pregunta y contesta. (AT2/2–3)

✕ *Speaking and interacting with others, Level C*

Speaking. Working in pairs, get pupils to ask each other what they are buying for the people in pictures a–e at the bottom of page 14.

Starter 2

Aim: To recap indirect object pronouns.

Ask pupils to unscramble the following two sentences:

1 *Compro camiseta una le*
2 *Un CD le compro*

What do the sentences mean? Point out that *le* can mean him or her.

3a Escribe el orden en que se menciona el carácter de las personas. (1–6) (AT1/3) [8L3]

✕ *Listening for information and instructions, Level C*

Listening. Pupils listen to the recording and write down the order in which the personality of each person is mentioned.

Answers

1 f   2 c   3 d   4 e   5 a   6 b

➕ Listen to the recording again and write down whether the person being described is female or male. Aim: To encourage pupils to distinguish between the adjectival endings.

5 Unos regalos

Tapescript

1 Pili es sociable.
2 Marta es una persona muy seria.
3 Julio es un chico muy simpático.
4 Elisa hace mucho deporte, es muy deportista.
5 Belén está siempre al teléfono. Es muy habladora.
6 Mercedes es tranquila.

3b Escucha otra vez y empareja los nombres con los dibujos en **3a**. (AT1/3) [8L3]

✚ *Listening for information and instructions, Level C*

Listening. Ask pupils to listen to the recording again and match the names with the drawings.

Answers

Pili-f Marta-c Julio-d Elisa-e Belén-a Mercedes-b

4 Con tu compañero/a, describe el carácter de tus compañeros/as de clase. (AT2/2–3) [8W4]

✚ *Speaking to convey information, Level C/D*

Speaking. Working in pairs, pupils use activity **3a** to help them discuss the personalities of some of their classmates.

5 Empareja las personas con los regalos. (AT3/2)

✚ *Reading for information/instructions, Level D*

Reading. Pupils match the personalities 1–5 with suitable presents a–e.

Answers

1 b 2 e 3 c 4 a 5 d

6 Describe a cinco de tus amigos y elige un regalo ideal para cada uno. Utiliza un diccionario. (AT4/3–4) [8W4; 8S6]

✚ *Exchange information/ideas, Level B–D*

Writing. Pupils write down what five of their friends are like, and choose a suitable present for them. Encourage them to look up possible presents in the dictionary.

Plenary

Ask a volunteer to tell you what the indirect object pronouns are in Spanish. What do they mean (me, you, him, her). Are they placed before the verb or after the verb in Spanish (before), and in English (after)?

Ask everyone to think of an example and take feedback.

Cuaderno A, page 7

1 Busca los nombres de seis regalos y escribe las palabras debajo de los dibujos apropiados. (AT3/1)

✚ *Reading for information/instructions, Level A*

Reading. Pupils use the six pictures as clues and look for the six presents in the wordsearch. Write these words down by the appropriate picture.

Answers

C	A	M	I	S	E	T	A	L	G	O	L	F
H	I	C	O	J	E	D	G	N	A	M	P	O
O	N	A	B	U	V	L	O	D	I	L	C	A
C	H	I	C	O	Í	U	R	A	M	B	U	L
A	C	U	R	E	D	I	R	C	R	O	P	U
L	G	A	L	L	E	T	A	S	P	O	R	O
A	M	O	R	B	O	M	B	O	N	E	S	A
T	E	L	É	F	O	N	O	M	Ó	V	I	L

1 gorra   2 camiseta   3 bonbones
4 galletas   5 teléfono móvil   6 vídeo

2 Empareja las descripciones con las personas. (AT3/3)

✚ *Reading for information/instructions, Level D*

Reading. Pupils match the descriptions 1–6 with the people a–f.

Answers

1 d 2 b 3 a 4 f 5 e 6 c

3 ¿Qué compra Paloma a su familia para la Navidad? Mira el dibujo y contesta a las preguntas. (AT4/2)

✚ *Exchange information/ideas, Level B*

Writing. Pupils look at the pictures and answer questions 1–4.

Answers

1 Le compra un CD.
2 Le compra un vídeo.
3 Le compra una camiseta.
4 Le compra una gorra.

Hojas de trabajo, Resource and Assessment File, pages 5 and 6

Cards for pairwork featuring items of toiletry and gifts: pupils match the pictures to the correct words.

6 Muchas gracias por el regalo

(Pupil's Book pages 16–17)

Main topics

- Writing a thank you letter
- Choosing an introduction
- Giving your thanks
- Saying what you like/don't like about the present
- Choosing an ending

Key Framework objectives

- Language and text types 8T3 (Launch)
- Dictionary use 8T4 (Launch)
- Text as model and source 8T6 (Launch)

Key language

Querido/a(s)/¡Hola!

amigo/a(s)	*familia*
tío/a(s)	*primo/a(s)*
abuelo/a(s)	

Muchas gracias por

el regalo	*el póster*
el dinero	*la foto*
el CD	*el llavero*
la camiseta	*la invitación*

Es (muy) (bastante) …

interesante	*bueno/a*
fantástico/a	*malo/a*
aburrido/a	

Me encanta/Me gusta/No me gusta/Lo/La detesto
Eres/Sois …

simpático/a(s)	*gracioso/a(s)*
antipático/a(s)	*cruel(es)*

Escríbeme pronto	*Hasta pronto*
Recuerdos a todos	*No me escribas nunca más*
Saludos	*Besos*
Abrazos	*Adiós*

Resources

Cassette A, side 1
CD 1, track 13
Cuaderno A, page 8
Hojas de trabajo, Resource and Assessment File, pages 5 and 6 (*una camiseta, un llavero, una gorra, dinero*)

Starter 1

Aim: Grouping adjectives under positive and negative headings.

Write the following adjectives on the board or prepare an OHT. Ask pupils to list them under 'good' and 'bad' and then write down what these adjectives mean. Encourage pupils to deduce meaning of unknown words.

interesante, aburrido, fantástico, gracioso, antipático, muy amable, poco amable, bueno, malo

1a Escucha y lee. Elige las opciones apropiadas para Alejandro, Paulina y Fran. (AT1/2) [8T3]

✉ *Listening for information and instructions, Level D*

Listening. Ask pupils to write down the three names Alejandro, Paulina, Fran and the numbers 1–7 for each name. They should produce a grid in which the names are the vertical option and the numbers the horizontal. Pupils write down the correct option for 1–7 next to each name. Point out that there may be more than one option for each person. Suggestion: If necessary, play the recording for each person twice.

R For lower ability pupils, photocopy the page and let pupils write the initial of the person next to each option or do it as a class exercise.

Answers

Alejandro: 1 Queridos (**e**) abuelos **2** Gracias por (**c**) el CD **3** Es muy (**c**) bueno **4** (**b**) Me gusta mucho **5** Sois (**c**) muy amables **6** (**b**) Hasta pronto (**d**) Besos (**c**) abrazos
Paulina: 1 Querida (**c**) tía **2** Gracias por (**d**) la camiseta **3** Es muy (**d**) bonita **4** (**a**) Me encanta **5** Eres (**c**) muy amable **6** (**e**) Recuerdos a todos (**c**) Saludos
Fran: 1 ¡Hola! (**d**) primo **2** Gracias por (**f**) la foto **3** Es (**g**) horrible **4** (**c**) No me gusta nada **5** Eres (**d**) antipático **6** (**f**) No me escribe nunca más (**h**) Adiós

Tapescript

Queridos abuelos:
Gracias por el CD de Limp Bizkit. Es muy bueno. Me gusta mucho. Sois muy amables. Hasta pronto. Besos y abrazos, Alejandro

Querida tía
Gracias por la camiseta. Es muy bonita. Me encanta. Eres muy amable. Recuerdos a todos. Saludos, Paulina

¡Hola, primo!
Gracias por la foto. Es horrible. No me gusta nada. Eres antipático. No me escribas nunca más. Adiós, Fran

1b Elige regalos para tu compañero/a. ¿Qué piensa de cada regalo? (AT2/3)

✉ *Speaking about feelings/opinions, Level C/D*

Speaking. Ask pupils to work in pairs taking turns to answer. Each pupil chooses presents for their partner. The partner then has to say what he/she thinks about the presents.

1c Mira la postal en **1a** otra vez y escribe una similar. (AT4/2) [8T6]

✕ *Writing for personal contact, Level C/D*

Writing. Pupils use the card in activity **1a** to help them compose their own.

🖰 ICT activity

Wordprocessing. Ask pupils to work in pairs and compose two thank you letters. One for something they like and one for something they don't like.

➕ You could print out extra copies of each letter and cut it up into six or seven parts. Put it into an envelope and swap the letters with another pair. Pupils then see if they can put them back together again.

Starter 2 [8T4]

Aim: Looking words up in the glossary.

Get pupils to have a quick look at pages 133–141 (the glossary). Ask them what the glossary is for. Look for answers like: Looking up unknown words, checking spellings of words you are unsure about, checking the gender of words, etc.

Put up about 6 words on an OHT or the board and ask pupils to work with a partner using the glossary to answer:

What do these mean? Are they spelled correctly (build in a deliberate error)? Are they masculine or feminine?

los consejos; el corazón; amarillo; casa; playa; dinero

Take feedback on answers.

2a Empareja las cartas con los dibujos. Utiliza un diccionario. (AT3/3) [8T3]

✕ *Reading for information/instructions, Level D*

Reading. Pupils match letters a–c with drawings 1–3.

Answers

a 2	b 1	c 3

2b Empareja las frases con las personas apropiadas: Tío Martín, Carlos, Emilia, Valentín, Luisa o Carmen. (AT3/4) [8T3]

✕ *Reading for information/instructions, Level D*

Reading. Pupils match sentences 1–6 with each of the people mentioned in the three letters.

Answers

1 Luisa **2** Emilia **3** tío Martín **4** Carlos **5** Valentín
6 Carmen

2c Recibes una invitación de tu amigo/a español(a). Escribe una respuesta (utiliza las cartas en **2a** para ayudarte). (AT4/3–4) [8T6]

✕ *Writing for personal contact, Level C/D*

Writing. Pupils acknowledge receipt of an invitation and answer whether they will accept or not. You may wish to support them by supplying a writing frame.

🖰 ICT activity

Wordprocessing. Ask pupils to wordprocess their letter. Make corrections which they can then incorporate into their work before making a print out.

Plenary.

Ask pupils to work in pairs and to write down three things they have learnt about writing a letter in Spanish. Write down four useful phrases that can be used in a letter.

Cuaderno A, page 8

1 Lee las cartas y rellena el cuadro. (AT3/3) [8T2, 3]

✕ *Reading for information/instructions, Level D*

Reading. Pupils read the three letters and fill in the grid with the appropriate information.

Answers

	What does she receive?	Who from?	What is the present like?	Does she like it?
Sofía	money	grandparents	practical	yes
Rosa	t-shirt	aunt	pretty	yes
Clara	photo	David	horrible	no

2a Recibes una invitación de tu amigo español. Contesta a las preguntas. (AT3/3) [8T2, 3]

✕ *Reading for information/instructions, Level D*

Reading. Pupils look at the invitation from a Spanish friend and answer questions 1–5 in English.

Answers

1 César **2** 3 weeks **3** September **4** very pretty
5 a swimming pool

2b Escribe una carta para aceptar la invitación. (AT4/3–4) [8T6]

✕ *Establish personal contact, Level C*

Writing. Pupils use the template provided to help them write a letter back accepting the invitation.

Hojas de trabajo, Resource and Assessment File, pages 5 and 6

Cards for pairwork featuring items of toiletry and gifts: pupils match the pictures to the correct words.

Resumen y Prepárate

(Pupil's Book pages 18–19)

Resumen

This is a checklist of language covered in Module 1. There is a comprehensive *Resumen* list for Module 1 in the Pupil's Book (page 18) and a *Resumen* test sheet in Cuaderno A (page 12).

Key Framework objectives

● Substituting and adding 8S6 (Reinforcement)

1 ¿Cómo son los jóvenes? Escucha y empareja los nombres con los dibujos. (AT1/3) [8L3]

✉ *Listening for information and instructions, Level C*

Listening. Pupils listen to the recording and match the names with pictures a–d.

Answers

1 Vicente **c**	2 Conchita **a**	3 Sebastián **d**	4 Manuela **b**

Tapescript

1 – ¿Cómo eres Vicente?
 – Soy bastante alto y soy moreno.
 – ¿De qué color son tus ojos?
 – Son marrones.
2 – ¿Cómo es tu pelo, Conchita?
 – Tengo el pelo castaño.
 – ¿De qué color son tus ojos?
 – Tengo los ojos verdes.
 – ¿Eres alta?
 – No, no soy alta. Soy baja.
3 – Sebastián, ¿cómo es tu pelo?
 – Tengo el pelo corto y rizado.
 – ¿De qué color son tus ojos?
 – Tengo los ojos marrones.
 – ¿Eres alto o bajo?
 – Soy bastante alto.
4 – ¿De qué color son tu ojos, Manuela?
 – Tengo los ojos azules.
 – ¿Cómo es tu pelo?
 – Soy pelirroja y tengo el pelo largo y rizado.
 – ¿Eres alta?
 – No soy ni alta ni baja.

2 Mira los dibujos. Con tu compañero/a pregunta y contesta. (AT2/3)

✉ *Speaking and interacting with others, Level C*

Speaking. Working in pairs, pupils take it in turns to ask and answer questions about things they need.

3a Empareja las frases con los dibujos. (AT3/2)

✉ *Reading for information/instructions, Level C*

Reading. Pupils match sentences 1–5 with drawings a–e.

Prepárate

A revision test to give practice for the test itself at the end of the module.

Resources

Cassette A, side 1
CD 1, track 14
Cuaderno A, pages 9, 10, 11 and 12.
Skills, Resource and Assessment File, page 8
Resumen, Resource and Assessment File, page 9

Answers

1 c	2 b	3 e	4 d	5 a

3b Lee las frases en **3a** otra vez y nombra las personas en cada dibujo. (AT3/2)

✉ *Reading for information/instructions, Level C*

Reading. Pupils read sentences 1–5 in activity **3a** again and say who the people are in each drawing.

Answers

a – A Adolfo, B Nicolás
b – A Diego, B Federico
c – A Gabriel, B Agustín
d – A Claudia, B Almudena
e – B Susana, A Pepita

4 Escribe una carta dando las gracias por un regalo. (AT4/3–4) [8S6]

✉ *Writing for personal contact, Level C/D*

Writing. Pupils write a thank-you letter.

Cuaderno A, page 9

Repaso

1 Contesta a las preguntas sobre ti. (AT3/2, AT4/2–3) [8W5]

✉ *Writing to exchange information/ideas, Level C*

Reading and writing: Pupils answer questions 1–9 with information about themselves.

2 Lee el fichero de Raúl. Rellena el fichero en blanco con los detalles de una persona famosa. (AT3/2, AT4/2)

✉ *Writing imaginatively, Level C*

Reading and writing: Pupils look at Raúl's details on the form and then fill in the blank form with another famous person's details.

3 Escribe *hace falta* o *hacen falta* en los espacios para completar las frases. [8W4]

✕ *Knowing about language*

Writing. Pupils write hace falta or hacen falta in the gaps to complete sentences 1–8.

Answers

1 hace falta	**2** hace falta	**3** hacen falta	**4** hace falta
5 hacen falta	**6** hace falta	**7** hace falta	**8** hacen falta

Cuaderno A, page 10

Gramática 1

1 Write five sentences using the words from the grid. [8W4]

✕ *Knowing about language*

Writing. Comparatives: Pupils write five personal sentences using words from the grid.

2 Write five sentences using the words in the grid. [8W4]

✕ *Knowing about language*

Writing. Superlatives: Pupils write five personal sentences using the words in the grid.

Cuaderno A, page 11

Gramática 2

1a Complete the sentences with the correct words. [8W4]

✕ *Knowing about language*

Answers

1 tío/abuelo/amigo **2** abuelos/padres/primos
3 abuelas/hermanas **4** tía/madre **5** abuelo/amigo/tío
6 madre/tía **7** padres/primos/abuelos
8 amigo/tío/abuelo **9** primos/abuelos/padres
10 hermanas/abuelas

1b Complete the sentences with the correct words.

✕ *Knowing about language*

Writing. Nouns: Pupils complete sentences 1–4 with words from the box.

Answers

1 Éste **2** Ésta **3** Éstas **4** Éstos

2 Complete the sentences with the appropriate words.

✕ *Knowing about language*

Writing. Object pronouns: Pupils complete sentences 1–4 with the appropriate object pronouns.

Answers

1 le **2** le **3** te **4** me

Skills, Resource and Assessment File, page 8 (Genders)

1

Answers

Masculine	Meaning	Feminine	Meaning
hermano	brother	hermana	sister
amigo	friend (m)	amiga	friend (f)
tío	uncle	tía	aunt
primo	cousin (m)	prima	cousin (f)
abuelo	grandfather	abuela	grandmother
hijo	son	hija	daughter

2

Answers

Word	Meaning 1	Meaning 2
a hermanos	brothers	brothers and sisters
b amigos	friends (m)	friends (m and f)
c tíos	uncles	aunts and uncles
d primos	cousins (m)	cousins (m and f)
e abuelos	grandfathers	grandparents (m and f)
f hijos	sons	sons and daughters

3a

Answers

One meaning

3b

Answers

Sisters

4

Answers

Masculine	Meaning	Feminine	Meaning
el padre		la madre	
el póster		la ciudad	
el regalo		la camiseta	

5

Answer

> The article:
> el = masculine
> la = feminine

6

Answers

Masculine	Meaning	Feminine	Meaning
el padre	the father	la madre	the mother
el póster	the poster	la ciudad	the city
el regalo	the gift	la camiseta	the t-shirt

7

Answers

Masculine	Meaning	Feminine	Meaning
un padre	a father	una madre	a mother
un póster	a poster	una ciudad	a city
un regalo	a gift	una camiseta	a t-shirt

Main topics

- This is an optional extension unit which reviews some of the key language of Module 1: Teenage magazine (*Mega Pop*)

Key Framework objectives

- Verb tenses (conditional) 9W5 (Launch)
- Understanding complex language 9T1 (Launch)

- Features for effect 9T2 (Launch)
- Authentic texts as source 9T3 (Launch)
- Daily life and young people 8C3 (Launch)

Resources

Cassette A, side 1
CD 1, track 15

Starter 1

Aim: To revise some of the language that comes up in the reading texts.

Write up *me gusta(n) …, me encanta(n) …* and *estoy loco/a por …* (You may have to explain the meaning of this). Give pupils two minutes to write a sentence beginning with each phrase.

1a Lee las cartas. Escribe el nombre apropiado para cada frase. (AT3/4) [9W5; 9T1, 2, 3; 8C3]

✂ *Reading for information/instructions, Level E*

Reading. Pupils read the letters and match 1–6 with the appropriate person.

Answers

1 Ana Luisa	**2** Wenceslas Vidal	**3** Pedro Gómez
4 Mireia y Isabel	**5** Carlos Sánchez	**6** Nieves Barreto

1b Elige una de las cartas. Con tu compañero/a, pregunta y contesta para adivinar quién eres. (AT2/3–4)

✂ *Speaking about feelings/opinions, Level D/E*

Speaking. Working in pairs, pupils choose to be one of the characters from letters 1–6. They then ask their partner questions to try and guess who they are.

Starter 2

Aim: Glossary practice.

Ask pupils to look up the following words in the dictionary:
horrible, aburrido, grande, madre, peine

1 Give the meaning. 2 Say whether it is a noun, verb or adjective. 3 If a noun, what gender is it?

2 Escucha y rellena la ficha. (AT1/3–4) [8L3]

✂ *Listening for information/instructions, Level D*

Listening. Pupils listen to the recording and fill in the grid.

Answers

	Martín	Noelia	Juan	Ester
edad	15	14	16	13
los animales		✓		
el cine		✓		✓
la música	✓		✓	
el baloncesto	✓			
el fútbol			✓	

Tapescript

1 ¡Hola! Me llamo Martín. Tengo 15 años. Me gustan la música y el baloncesto.

2 Me llamo Noelia. Tengo 14 años. Me encantan los animales y el cine.

3 Mi nombre es Juan. Tengo 16 años. Me gusta la música y me gusta el deporte, sobre todo el baloncesto y el fútbol. Soy un aficionado del Deportivo de La Coruña.

4 ¡Hola! Soy Ester. Tengo 13 años. Me gusta mucho el cine y mi actor preferido es Adam Sandler. Es muy divertido.

✚ You could play items 3 and 4 again and ask pupils if they can give you any extra information.

3 Escribe una carta a la revista *Mega Pop*. (AT4/3–4) [9T3]

✂ *Writing imaginatively, Level C–E*

Writing. Pupils use the example letter at the bottom of page 21 to help them write their own letter to the magazine *Mega Pop*.

Plenary

Ask pupils to list four things they have learnt in this Module and find the most useful, giving reasons. They then compare notes with a partner.

You could then go on to do a 'Find the Spanish for …' activity with pupils focusing on phrases that will be useful in their own writing. For example, I'm a fan of …, above all, I would like, plus the phrases highlighted in Starter 1 – I like, I love, I'm mad about.

Te toca a ti

(Pupil's Book pages 108–109)

● Self-access reading and writing at two levels

Key Framework objectives

● Question types 8S4 (Reinforcement)
● Famous people 8C2 (Reinforcement)

A Reinforcement

1 Paco, Barto y Carmela se presentan. Escribe una frase para cada dibujo. (AT4/3)

✖ *Exchange information/ideas, Level B/C*

Writing. Pupils write sentences to introduce each of the three people.

2a Empareja las preguntas con las respuestas. (AT3/3) [8S4]

✖ *Reading for information/instructions, Level C*

Reading. Pupils match the questions with the answers.

Answers

1 c	**2** f	**3** g	**4** a	**5** h	**6** b	**7** d	**8** e

2b Contesta a las preguntas de **2a** para ti. (AT4/3–4) [8S4]

✖ *Exchange information/ideas, Level D*

Writing. Pupils answer the questions in **2a** with their own information.

B Extension

1a Lee la ficha. ¿Verdad (✓) o mentira (✗) ? (AT3/3) [8C2]

✖ *Reading for information/instructions, Level D*

Reading. Pupils look at the card of Antonio Banderas and answer '*verdad*' (✓) o '*mentira*' (✗) for 1–8.

Answers

1 ✓	**2** ✓	**3** ✓	**4** ✓	**5** ✗	**6** ✗	**7** ✗	**8** ✓

1b Completa una ficha similar sobre otro actor o actriz. (AT4/3) [9T3]

✖ *Writing imaginatively, Level C/D*

Writing. Pupils make up their own form with personal information about another actor or actress.

2 ¿Qué regalos vas a comprar para los cumpleaños de tu familia y amigos y por qué? Copia y completa el cuadro. (AT4/2)

✖ *Exchange information/ideas, Level C/D*

Writing. Pupils copy the grid and fill in the information: family member, birthday, present they are going to buy for that person and their personal qualities.

3 Lee el correo electrónico y contesta a las preguntas. (AT3/4)

✖ *Reading for information/instructions, Level D*

Reading. Pupils read the e-mail and answer questions 1–8 in English.

Answers

1 Quito **2** 14 **3** 20th September **4** brown
5 black, long, straight **6** sociable, good sense of humour
7 active, sporty **8** tennis, basketball

módulo 2 — La comida

(Pupil's Book pages 24–41)

Unit	Key Framework objectives	PoS	Key language and Grammar
1 ¿Qué comes? (pp. 24–25) Saying what you have to eat Talking about meal times in Spain and the UK Talking about likes and dislikes	8S6 Substituting and adding [R] 8T4 Dictionary use [R]	2i report main points 2f adapt language for different contexts 4b communicating with native speakers 4c compare cultures 5e range of resources 5h use TL for real purposes	*¿Qué comes de (primer plato)?* *(No) Como (sopa).* *(No) Ceno (carne).* *(No) Tomo (fruta).* *¿Te gusta (el pescado/las patatas fritas)?* *Me encanta(n) …* *(No) Me gusta(n) …* *Odio …*
2 ¿Qué te gusta comer? (pp. 26–27) Saying what type of food you like Saying why you like it	8W1 Adding abstract words [L] 8L4 Extending sentences [L] 8W4 Word endings [R]	2a listen for gist and detail 2c ask and answer questions 2i report main points 3d use reference materials 4c compare cultures 5c express opinions 5e range of resources	Adjective agreements *sano/a(s)* *dulce(s)* *¿Qué tipo de comida te gusta?* *Me gusta/Prefiero la comida (rápida).* *¿Cuál es tu plato preferido?* *Mi plato preferido es …* *Porque es/son (nutritivo/a(s)).*
3 De compras (pp. 28–29) Buying fruit and vegetables Finding out how much things cost Quantities Prices (euros) Pronunciation practice: *ll, j,* short vowels	8L3 Relaying gist and detail [L] 8S6 Substituting and adding [R]	1a sounds and writing 2b pronunciation/ intonation 2i report main points 5e range of resources	*¿Qué desea?* *Deme (un cuarto kilo de (peras))* *¿Cuánto cuesta?* *Cuesta … euros.*
4 Cien gramos de jamón y una barra de pan (pp. 30–31) Buying food and drink in a shop Numbers 31–1000 Quantities	8L1 Listening for subtleties [L] 8L3 Relaying gist and detail [R]		Numbers 0–1000 *¿Qué desea?* *Una botella de limonada, 200 gramos de queso …* *¿Algo más? Sí, …* *No, nada más, gracias.*
5 ¡Que aproveche! (pp. 32–33) Saying that you are hungry and thirsty Ordering from a menu	8C5 Colloquialisms [L] 8W5 Verb tenses (future) [L] 8S5 Negative forms and words [R]	2e adapt language 2f adapt language for different contexts 4a working with authentic materials 4c compare cultures 5e range of resources	*Tener: tengo hambre/tengo sed* *¿Qué va(n) a tomar?* *Para mí (calamares).* *¿Qué va(n) a beber?* *Para él/ella (agua con gas).* *¿Va(n) a tomar algo más?* *No, nada más.*
6 La comida sana (pp. 34–35) Talking about healthy eating	8W5 Verbs (present) [R] 8S5 Negative forms and words [R] 8T3 Language and text types [R]	2e adapt language 2h scanning texts 4a working with authentic materials 5e range of resources 5f using the TL creatively 5h using TL for real purposes	The imperative: *come, bebe* Talking about frequency: *al, a la* *Come … todos los días.* *Bebe … algunas veces a la semana/algunas veces al mes.*

módulo 2 ∷ La comida

Unit	Key Framework objectives	PoS	Key language and Grammar
Resumen y Prepárate (pp. 36–37) Pupil's checklist and practice test	8T6 Text as model and source [R] 8L3 Relaying gist and detail [R]		
7 ¡Extra! ¡Feliz Navidad! (pp. 38–39) Optional unit: Christmas and New Year in Spain.	8C4 Poems/ jokes/ songs [L] 8S4 Question types [R] 8T3 Language and text types [R] 8T4 Dictionary use [R]	2h scanning texts 4c compare cultures 4d consider experiences in other countries 5d respond to different types of language 5g listening/reading for enjoyment	
Te toca a ti (pp. 110–111) Self-access reading and writing at two levels	8S5 Negative forms and words [R] 8C5 Colloquialisms [R]		

1 ¿Qué comes?
(Pupil's Book pages 24–25)

Main topics
- Saying what you have to eat
- Talking about meal times in Spain and the UK

Key Framework objectives
- Substituting and adding 8S6 (Reinforcement)
- Dictionary use 8T4 (Reinforcement)

Other aims
- Talking about likes and dislikes
- Pronunciation 'h'

Grammar
- *Me encanta(n) …*
- *Me gusta(n) …*
- *No me gusta(n) …*
- *Odio …*

Key language
¿Qué comes de primer plato?
¿Qué comes de segundo plato?
¿Qué tomas de postre?
(No) Como/Ceno/Tomo …

huevos	*fruta*
verduras	*tarta*
sopa	*pescado*
ensalada	*pollo*
carne	*patatas fritas*
helado	

Resources
Cassette A, side 2
CD 1, tracks 16 and 17
Cuaderno A, page 13
Starter 2 Resource and Assessment File, page 24
Hojas de trabajo, Resource and Assessment File, pages 26 and 27 (*los huevos, las verduras, la carne, el helado, el pescado, el pollo*)
Flashcards 1–7 and 15, 18 (*¡Listos! 1*)
OHTS 7 and 8

Starter 1 [8W4]

Aim: To talk about likes and dislikes in a different context.

Write on the board or prepare an OHT with: *me gusta(n), me encanta(n), no me gusta(n), odio.* Ask pupils to work in pairs and tell their partner two things they like (one of which could be something they really like) and two things they dislike (one of which could be something they really dislike). They could talk about school or after school/weekend activities. Go round the class. Throw a fluffy toy/ball to a pupil. They must then say one thing they like and one thing they dislike before throwing the toy back and so on.

Suggestion

Brainstorm session. Quickly see what pupils know about eating habits in Spain and then compare them with our own. If it hasn't been pointed out you could mention that the Spanish tend only to have a light breakfast: yoghurt or fruit, and then a more substantial snack at mid-morning, coffee and a pastry (10.00–11.00). Lunch is later, usually from 2.30 and is the main meal of the day – which is why it is called *la comida.* This is changing as fast food becomes more popular, and people tend not to have the long afternoon rest *(la siesta)* due to office hours becoming more 9–5 (they used to have a longer break during the day and work until later). Dinner is from 8.00–10.00 and tends to be lighter, for example soup and a salad.

Suggestion

Use flashcards 1–7 to introduce food. Ask your class to repeat the names of different foods with you. Do this a couple of times. Then hold up a flashcard and ask *¿Qué es?* etc.

Play a game. Turn or hide the cards so pupils can't see the pictures. They must try to guess what food card you are holding. Whoever guesses correctly is 'given' the card. You collect the cards in by trying to remember which card it is that each pupil is holding!

This is a good opportunity to practise the mute 'h' in *helado* and *huevos.*

Before going on to the listening activity, introduce *ensalada, fruta, tarta* and *patatas fritas.*

1a ¿Qué comida le gusta o no le gusta a Rodrigo? Escribe la letra del dibujo y marca con ✓ o ✗. (1–7) (AT1/3) [8L3]

✂ *Listening for information/instructions, Level C*

Listening. Pupils listen to the recording and write down the letter of the food mentioned. They put a tick next to it if the person likes it and a cross if the person dislikes it. Point out that there may be more than one food option.

Answers

```
1 d ✗ b ✓   2 c ✗   3 j ✓ k ✓   4 a ✓   5 i ✗ e ✓
6 g ✗ f ✓   7 h ✓
```

Tapescript

1 – ¿Te gusta la ensalada?
 – No, no me gusta la ensalada, prefiero las verduras.
2 – ¿Te gusta la sopa?
 – No me gusta la sopa.
3 – Rodrigo, ¿te gusta el pollo?
 – Sí, me gusta el pollo. El pollo con las patatas fritas.
4 – ¿Te gustan los huevos?
 – Me encantan los huevos.
5 – ¿Te gusta el pescado?
 – No, odio el pescado. Prefiero la carne.
6 – ¿Te gusta la fruta?
 – No me gusta la fruta. Prefiero el helado.
7 – ¿Te gusta la tarta?
 – Sí, me encanta.

1b Con tu compañero/a, pregunta y contesta. (AT2/2–3) [8S4]

✖ *Speaking about feelings/opinions, Level C*

Speaking. Working in pairs, pupils take it in turns to ask their partner if they like the food in activity **1a**.

ICT activity

Class survey. Pupils carry out a survey on food likes and dislikes. Get them to write down the above food and ask members of the class whether they like them or not. They keep a tally, ✓ for *sí* and ✗ for *no*. You could then use chart wizard in MS Excel to enter the data collected – make various foods the headings for each column and then produce a pie chart or bar chart of likes and dislikes. This will also work out percentages so pupils can write down their results or report back to the class. e.g.: *huevos: 60% les gustan, 40% no les gustan*, etc.

2a ¿Qué comen o cenan estas personas? Copia y completa el cuadro. (AT1/3) [8L3]

✖ *Listening for information and instructions, Level D*

Listening. Pupils listen to the recording and fill in the grid. Alternatively, ask pupils to simply write down the letters of each item of food mentioned.

Answers

Pablo a, c, d, k	Ester b, f, g, i	Rubén a, h	Patricia e, j

Tapescript

1 – ¿Qué comes de primer plato Pablo?
 – Como verduras de primer plato.
 – ¿Y de segundo plato?
 – Pollo y ensalada.
 – ¿Y de postre?
 – Como fruta.
2 – ¿Qué cenas, Ester?
 – De primer plato tomo sopa.
 – ¿Y qué tomas de segundo plato?

 – Tomo pescado, pescado con patatas fritas.
 – ¿Y de postre?
 – Tomo helado de postre.
3 – ¿Qué comes, Rubén?
 – Como verduras de primer plato.
 – ¿Y de segundo plato?
 – De segundo plato como carne.
 – ¿Y de postre?
 – No como postre.
4 – ¿Qué cenas Patricia?
 – Ceno huevos
 – ¿Y de postre?
 – Tomo tarta.

2b Con tu compañero/a, pregunta y contesta. (AT2/3–4) [8S4]

✖ *Speaking and interacting with others, Level C*

Speaking. Working in pairs, pupils use the grid in activity **2a** to ask their partner what they are having for each course.

Suggestion

Use the menu on OHTs 7 and 8 for colourful extra practice.

Starter 2

Revise some of the food vocabulary using *Resource and Assessment File*, page 24. Ask pupils to work out the anagrams and see who can finish first.

SOACDEP (*pescado*), SPOA (*sopa*), VEOSUH (*huevos*), SLDAAANE (*ensalada*), RATTA (*tarta*), LLOPO (*pollo*)

Reinforce the mute 'h' in *huevos* (also *helado*)

3a Lee el correo electrónico de Fátima. ¿Verdad (✓) o mentira (✗)? Utiliza un diccionario (AT3/4) [8T4]

✖ *Reading for information/instructions, Level D*

Reading. Pupils read Fátima's letter and write down true or false for numbers 1–7.

Answers

1 ✓	2 ✗	3 ✓	4 ✓	5 ✓	6 ✗	7 ✗

✚ Ask pupils to correct the answers that are false.

ICT activity

Set up an E-mail link with another school (be it in Spain or another Spanish class in an English school). For this exercise pupils could compare what they have to eat and at what time.

E-mail links enable pupils to use the language they have just learnt in a real situation. They also provide you with real reading and writing material.

3b Contesta al correo electrónico de Fátima. (AT4/1 and AT3/2) [8S6]

✖ *Writing for personal contact, Level A*

Writing. Ask pupils to answer Fátima's letter, copying the letter at the bottom of page 25 and filling in the blanks.

R Ask lower ability pupils to select appropriate vocabulary from the side and fill in the gaps.

Answers

1 doce **2** ensalada **3** sopa **4** pollo **5** patatas fritas **6** tarta **7** siete **8** nada **9** huevos **10** fruta

➕ 🖙 **ICT activity**

Wordprocessing. Get pupils to use the above letter to compose their own.

> *Plenary*
>
> Ask pupils what they have found out about meal times in Spain. How does it compare with their own?
>
> What do the Spanish like to eat? *¿Qué te gusta comer? Me gustan los huevos, no me gusta la carne.* Go around the class and take feedback.

Cuaderno A, page 13

1a Lee los globos, mira los dibujos y escribe los números en el cuadro. (AT3/3)

✖ *Reading for information/instructions, Level C*

Reading. Pupils look at the food, pictures 1–11, and the three speech bubbles with descriptions of what Fernando, Paco and Mari Luz eat. They write the numbers of what each person eats in the grid under *primer plato*, *segundo plato* and *postre*.

Answers

	primer plato	segundo plato	postre
Fernando	✗	4/6	10
Paco	1	5	✗
Mari Luz	2	5	11

1b Completa el cuadro y el globo sobre ti. (AT4/2–3) [8T6]

✖ *Exchange information/ideas, Level C/D*

Writing. Pupils fill in the speech bubble with information about what they usually eat.

Hojas de trabajo, Resource and Assessment File, pages 26 and 27

Cards for pairwork featuring various foods: pupils match the pictures to the correct words.

módulo 2

2 ¿Qué te gusta comer?
(Pupil's Book pages 26–27)

Main topics

- Saying what type of food you like
- Saying why you like it

Key Framework objectives

- Adding abstract words 8W1 (Launch)
- Connectives 8W2 (Launch)
- Word endings 8W4 (Reinforcement)
- Extending sentences 8L4 (Launch)

Grammar

- Agreement of adjectives
  -o, -a, -os, -as

Key language

¿Qué tipo de comida te gusta?
Me gusta/Prefiero la comida …
rápida   italiana
india   mexicana
china   vegetariana
¿Cuál es tu plato preferido?
Mi plato preferido es …
perritos calientes   gambas
chuletas   sardinas
flan
Porque es(está)/son(están) …
sano/a(s)   nutritivo/a(s)
delicioso/a(s)   dulce(s)
rico/a(s)   grasiento/a(s)

Resources

Cassette A, side 2
CD 1, tracks 18 and 19
Cuaderno A, page 14
Grammar, Resource and Assessment File, page 28
Flashcards 8–11

Starter 1 [8W4]

Aim: To revise the definite article.

Write the following words on the board. Ask pupils to fill in the blanks with the correct form of 'the'. You may wish to remind pupils that there are four ways to say 'the' in Spanish. What are they? See if pupils can tell you and write them on the board.

1 … *comida italiana*   2 … *vegetariana*
3 … *perritos calientes*   4 … *flan*   5 … *chuletas*

Add more if you wish.

Suggestion

Introduce food items with flashcards 8–11 and introduce the cognate *las sardinas* (no flashcard).

1a ¿Qué tipo de comida les gusta a las personas? (1–5) (AT1/3) [8L3]

✖ *Listening for information/instructions, Level E*

Listening. Pupils listen to the recording and write down what type of food each person likes to eat.

Answers

1 d   2 c   3 e   4 f   5 a

Tapescript

1 – *¿Qué tipo de comida te gusta a ti?*
   – *Adoro la comida italiana, especialmente los macarrones y los espaguetis.*
2 – *¿Qué tipo de comida te gusta a ti?*
   – *Pues, a mí me gusta la comida china, el arroz, los fideos, todo tipo de comida china.*
3 – *¿Qué tipo de comida te gusta?*
   – *Me encanta la comida mexicana. Adoro los tacos, las tortillas, el guacamole.*
4 – *¿Qué tipo de comida te gusta?*
   – *Soy vegetariana. No como carne ni pescado. Prefiero verduras.*
5 – *¿Qué tipo de comida te gusta?*
   – *Me gusta mucho la comida rápida. Me encantan las hamburguesas.*

1b Haz un sondeo. Pregunta a tus compañeros/as de clase. Copia y rellena el cuadro. (AT2/3–4) [8S4]

✖ *Speaking about feelings/opinions, Level C/D*

Speaking. Get pupils to copy the grid on page 26 and ask their class what foods they like/dislike.

ICT activity

MS Excel. Use 'Wizard' to produce a pie chart or a bar chart showing class results.

2a Escucha y elige las opiniones apropiadas de Martín para cada plato. (1–5) Utiliza un diccionario. (AT1/3) [8W1; 8L3]

✖ *Listening for information/instructions, Level D*

Listening. Pupils listen to the recording and write down what Martín thinks of each dish. Remind them to use the box at the top of page 27 to help them.

Answers

1 ricos (los perritos calientes)   2 deliciosas (las chuletas)
3 dulce (el flan)   4 deliciosas (las gambas)
5 nutritivas (las sardinas)

2 ¿Que te gusta comer?

➕ Ask pupils to listen to the recording again and tell which dish he isn't really keen on.

Tapescript

1 – ¿Cuál es tu plato preferido, Martín?
 – Adoro los perritos calientes. Están muy ricos.
2 – ¿Te gustan las chuletas?
 – Me encantan las chuletas. Son deliciosas.
3 – ¿Cuál es tu postre preferido?
 – Mi postre preferido es el flan.
 – ¿Por qué?
 – Porque es dulce. Me gustan las cosas dulces.
4 – ¿Te gustan las gambas?
 – Me encantan las gambas, especialmente al ajillo. Son deliciosas.
5 – ¿Te gustan las sardinas?
 – No me gustan mucho, pero son muy nutritivas.

2b Con tu compañero/a, pregunta y contesta. (AT2/3–4) [8W1, 4; 8L4]

✖ *Speaking and interacting with others, Level C/D*

Speaking. Working in pairs, pupils ask their partner which dish they prefer and why. *¿Cuál es tu plato preferido? ¿Por qué? Mi plato preferido es … porque es (está)/son (están) …*

You will need to explain that the adjective *rico/a(s)* takes *está/están*.

➕ Circular memory game. Ask pupils to sit in a circle. You start off saying something you like: *Me gustan las peras.* The next person says what they like and what you like: *Me gustan los plátanos y las peras,* and so on. If someone makes a mistake or can't remember then they are out.

Starter 2 [8W4]

Aim: To revise adjective agreement. Dictionary practice.

Write on the board or prepare an OHT of the following:

Las chuletas son …, los huevos son …, el flan es …, la tarta es …

deliciosas, nutritivos, dulce, rica.

Ask pupils to choose the correct adjective for each.

Ask them why they chose the adjectives they did. What do these sentences mean in English? Get them to look up any words they don't know in a dictionary.

You may wish to remind pupils before starting that they must use the verb *estar* with *rico/a(s)*.

3a Empareja los dibujos con las descripciones. (AT3/4)

✖ *Reading for information/instructions, Level D*

Reading. Pupils match the pictures with the appropriate description a and b. You will have to teach *los mariscos* (seafood)

Answers

1 c 2 a 3 b

3b Contesta a las preguntas. (AT3/4)

✖ *Reading for information/instructions, Level D*

Reading. Pupils read the two letters and answer questions 1–5 in English.

Answers

1 paella 2 rice, seafood, fish 3 nutritious 4 mexican 5 tacos with guacomole

3c Escribe frases sobre la comida y los platos que te gustan y no te gustan. (AT4/3–4) [8W2; 8L4]

✖ *Exchange information/ideas, Level B–D*

Writing. Pupils write down what sort of food they like, which is their favourite dish and why.

Plenary

Ask pupils to work in pairs to answer the following questions about nouns and their adjectives.

1 If a noun is masculine and singular what ending will its adjective have (*o* or *e*)? Think of an example from the adjectives you have just met. e.g. *sano, dulce*
2 If a noun is masculine and plural what ending will its adjective take (*os/es*)? Think of an example: *sanos, dulces*
3 Do the same for feminine singular and feminine plural. Give examples.

En casa

Personal dossier. Get pupils to cut out pictures from a magazine or draw a picture of their favourite dish. They then write down what their favourite dish is and why. They could also write down what the favourite dish is for their mother, father, brother, sister, favourite pet, etc. and give their opinion of this person's favourite dish? Do they like it/dislike it? Why?

🔊 ICT activity

Keep a personal record on recording or CD. Up-date this on a regular basis. This is quite a good way for pupils to notice an improvement in their Spanish as they work their way through the course.

Cuaderno A, page 14

1 Empareja las frases. (AT3/3) [8S2, 5]

Reading for information/instructions, Level C

Reading. Pupils match the sentences. Point out that they should think about whether the food in 1–5 is singular or plural/feminine or masculine before matching them with the reasons a–e (adjectives).

Answers

1 b/c	**2** a	**3** e	**4** d	**5** c/b

2a Empareja los globos con los dibujos. (AT 3/3) [8S2, 5]

Reading for information/instructions, Level C

Reading. Pupils match the speech bubbles a–d with the pictures 1–4.

Answers

a 2	**c** 1	**b** 4	**d** 3

2b ¿Verdad (✓) o mentira (✗)? (AT3/3) [8S2, 5]

Reading for information/instructions, Level C

Reading. Pupils do a true or false exercise 1–8, based on the speech bubbles a–d in **1a**.

Answers

1 ✓	**2** ✓	**3** ✓	**4** ✗	**5** ✗	**6** ✓	**7** ✗	**8** ✗

Grammar, Resource and Assessment File, page 28

How to talk about likes and dislikes

1

Pupils look at the prompts to decide on the correct form of the verb *gustar* and write sentences about their opinions.

Answers

> **a** No me gusta el pescado.
> **b** Me gustan los tomates.
> **c** Me encanta el queso.
> **d** No me gustan las hamburguesas.
> **e** Me gusta la carne.

2

Pupils write their own opinions using *gusta/gustan*.

Using adjectives

3

Pupil's fill in a grid with the correct forms of the adjectives according to whether they are masculine (sing. or pl.) or femenine (sing. or pl.).

Answers

Masculine	Masc. pl	Feminine	Fem. pl	Meaning
delicioso	deliciosos	deliciosa	deliciosas	delicious
dulce	dulces	dulce	dulces	sweet
grasiento	grasientos	grasienta	grasientas	fatty
nutritivo	nutritivos	nutritiva	nutritivas	nutritious
rico	ricos	rica	ricas	tasty
sano	sanos	sana	sanas	healthy

4

Pupils are given various foods (masc./fem./sing./pl.) plus an adjective and must make a sentence, using the correct form of each adjective.

Answers

> **a** El arroz es nutritivo.
> **b** Las verduras son sanas.
> **c** Los caramelos son dulces.
> **d** La hamburguesa es grasienta.
> **e** El flan está rico.

5

Pupils now write sentences of their own using the rules they have practised.

Main topics

- Buying fruit and vegetables
- Finding out how much things cost

Key Framework objectives

- Substituting and adding 8S6 (Reinforcement)
- Relaying gist and detail 8L3 (Launch)

Other aims

- Quantities
- Prices in euros
- Pronunciation practice: *ll, j*, short vowels

Key language

¿Qué desea?
Deme … de …
cuarto kilo   medio kilo

un kilo	*dos kilos*
los plátanos	*las naranjas*
las peras	*las uvas*
los tomates	*las patatas*
las lechugas	*las cebollas*
¿Cuánto cuesta?	
Cuesta … euros.	

Resources

Cassette A, side 2
CD 1, tracks 20, 21, 22 and 23
Cuaderno A, page 15
Hojas de trabajo, Resource and Assessment File, pages 26 and 27 (*las uvas, las naranjas, los plátanos, las patatas, una lechuga*)
Flashcards 12–16
OHTs 9 and 10

Starter 1

Aim: To practise numbers 1–100.

Throw a ball to a pupil and say the number 1. They throw it back saying the number 2. Go round the class, speeding up the pace. If someone drops the ball go back to one. You may want to practise counting in tens if you are going to go up to 100.

Suggestion

At the time of writing, Great Britain has not joined the Euro so some pupils may be unfamiliar with the coins and notes. Take some coins in to show your class. Do some coin rubbing!

Use Flashcards 12–16 to help you introduce the food in this unit. There are no flashcards for *las patatas, los tomates* or *las naranjas*.

You could also use OHTs 9 and 10 to help introduce the food and vocabulary.

1a Escucha y escribe las frutas y verduras en el orden correcto. (1–8) (AT1/1)

✖ *Listening for information/instructions, Level A*

Listening. Pupils listen to the recording and write down the letters of the fruit and vegetables in the correct order.

Answers

1 c   2 f   3 e   4 a   5 h   6 b   7 d   8 g

Tapescript

1 *las peras*
2 *las patatas*

3 *los tomates*
4 *los plátanos*
5 *las cebollas*
6 *las naranjas*
7 *las uvas*
8 *las lechugas*

ICT activity

Fun with texts. Input the food vocabulary in this unit. Use scrambler/enigma (jumbles/codes) to practise and reinforce spelling.

1b Escucha otra vez y repite. Pon atención a la pronunciación. (AT1/1) [7L1]

✖ *Knowing about language*

Listening/Speaking. Pupils listen to the recording and repeat the words. Remind them that vowels are short, *ll* has a 'yeh' sound and *j* is a guttural sound from the back of the throat.

Tapescript

As for activity 1a.

2a Escucha los diálogos. ¿Qué compran los clientes y en qué cantidades? (1–4) (AT1/4) [8W1; 8L3]

✖ *Listening for information/instructions, Level D*

Listening. Pupils listen to the recording and write down what the customers buy and in what quantities. In some of the conversations the customers will buy more than one thing.

Suggestions

1 Listen to the recording twice. Once for the item being bought and the second time for quantities.

2 Ask pupils to write down the letter of the item being bought. Take these from the picture in activity 1a. This way lower ability pupils can concentrate on the listening and not worry about the writing as well.

Answers

1 1kg naranjas	**2** $\frac{1}{2}$ kg peras, 1kg tomates
3 $\frac{1}{4}$ kg plátanos, $\frac{1}{4}$ kg uvas	**4** 1$\frac{1}{2}$ kg cebollas, 2 kg patatas

Tapescript

1 – Buenos días. ¿Qué desea?
 – Un kilo de naranjas.
 – ¿Algo más?
 – No, nada más, gracias.
2 – Buenos días, señora. ¿Qué desea?
 – Medio kilo de peras.
 – Muy bien, medio kilo de peras. ¿Algo más?
 – Sí, un kilo de tomates.
 – Un kilo de tomates. Tome usted.
3 – Buenas tardes, señor. ¿Qué desea?
 – ¿Tiene plátanos?
 – Sí, hay plátanos.
 – Pues, un cuarto kilo de plátanos.
 – ¿Algo más?
 – Sí, un cuarto kilo de uvas.
 – Tome usted, un cuarto kilo de plátanos y un cuarto kilo de uvas.
4 – Buenas tardes. ¿Qué desea?
 – Un kilo y medio de cebollas y dos kilos de patatas.
 – Tome usted, kilo y medio de cebollas y dos kilos de patatas. ¿Algo más?
 – Nada más, gracias.

2b Mira los dibujos. Con tu compañero/a, pregunta y contesta. (AT2/3–4) [8S6]

✖ *Speaking and interacting with others, Level C/D*

Speaking. Working in pairs, pupils take it in turns to ask for the items in the drawings. Note: you will need to teach *las zanahorias* (carrots) and *las manzanas* (apples).

✚ Play a game to practise vocabulary from this and the previous unit. Ask pupils to sit in a circle. Each pupil is given the name of a different fruit or vegetable. Stand in the centre of the circle and call out the name of one fruit/vegetable three times as quickly as possible. The pupil who has this fruit or vegetable must shout it out once, before the teacher has called it out three times. If they succeed, they keep their seat. If not, they must give up their seat to the person in the middle.

Starter 2

Aim: Listening skills.

Ask pupils to listen to the recording again from activity **2b**. A useful exercise if this was broken down into sections at the last listening. This time play it through without stopping. Ask pupils to write down what is being bought and the quantity. You could point out that they have already heard this recording and that the purpose of this exercise is to reinforce what they have already learnt. This should give pupils further confidence knowing that the language is not totally new.

3a Mira el dibujo. ¿Qué quieren comprar y cuánto cuesta? (1–6) (AT1/2) [8L3]

✖ *Listening for information/instructions, Level B*

Listening. Pupils look at the drawing at the top of page 29 and listen to the recording. Ask them to write down what the people in 1–6 want to buy and how much they have to pay.

Suggestion

You may wish to break this down as with activity **2a**. Ask pupils first to write down what is being bought and the quantity. Then play the recording again and get them to write down how much each costs.

Answers

1 1kg tomates/3 euros	**2** 1kg patatas/ 2 euros
3 1kg naranjas/ 3 euros	**4** 1kg uvas/4 euros
5 1kg plátanos/2 euros	**6** una lechuga/1 euro

Tapescript

1 – ¿Cuánto cuesta un kilo de tomates?
 – Cuesta 3 euros.
2 – ¿Cuánto cuesta un kilo de patatas?
 – Cuesta 2 euros.
3 – ¿Cuánto cuesta un kilo de naranjas?
 – Cuesta 3 euros.
4 – ¿Cuánto cuesta un kilo de uvas?
 – Cuesta 4 euros.
5 – ¿Cuánto cuesta un kilo de plátanos?
 – Cuesta 2 euros.
6 – ¿Cuánto cuesta una lechuga?
 – Cuesta un euro.

3b Con tu compañero/a, pregunta y contesta. (AT2/3–4) [8S4, 6]

✖ *Speaking and interacting with others, Level C/D*

Speaking. Working in pairs, pupils take it in turns to ask and answer questions about the fruit and vegetables in the drawing.

4 Escribe un diálogo entre un/a cliente y un/a tendero/a en el mercado. (AT4/3–4) [8S6]

✉ *Exchange information/ideas, Level B–D*

Writing. Ask pupils to write a dialogue between a customer and a stallholder.

🔊 ICT activity

➕ *Recording.* Ask pupils to work with a partner and record their dialogues on recording (If possible, set this up before your pupils arrive in a relatively quiet part of the room!) If you have access to a student/language assistant/A-level pupil, get them to run this activity. When the recordings are finished, play them back to the class once so that everyone can hear themselves, and then a second time. On this second go, ask pupils to write down what it is being bought, the quantities and how much they cost.

Plenary

Go round the room and ask pupils to count in tens up to 100. From 100 they should count in 100's.

Ask pupils how to say:
How much does it cost? (*¿Cuánto cuesta?*)

What would you like? (*¿Qué desea?*)

Do you have? (*¿Tiene …?*)

Anything else? (*¿Algo más?*)

Cuaderno A, page 15

1 Empareja las palabras con los dibujos. (AT3/1)

✉ *Reading for information/instructions, Level B*

Reading. Pupils match the fruit and vegetables (1–8) with the pictures (a–h).

Answers

1 e	2 f	3 b	4 g	5 d	6 a	7 h	8 c

2a Completa el diálogo. (AT4/2)

✉ *Exchange information/ideas, Level B*

Writing. Pupils complete the dialogue by looking at the picture symbols and choosing appropriate words from activity **1**.

Answers

naranjas	plátanos	plátanos	cebollas	patatas

2b Escribe una conversación similar. Cambia los productos y las cantidades. (AT4/2–3) [8T2; 8C5]

✉ *Exchange information/ideas, Level C*

Writing. Pupils use the dialogue in activity **2a** as a template and write a similar one, changing the products and quantities.

Hojas de trabajo, Resource and Assessment File, pages 26 and 27

Cards for pairwork featuring various foods: pupils match the pictures to the correct words.

4 Cien gramos de jamón y una barra de pan (Pupil's Book pages 30–31)

Main topics

- Buying food and drink in a shop
- Numbers 31–1000
- Quantities

Key Framework objectives

- Listening for subtleties 8L1 (Launch)
- Relaying gist and detail 8L3 (Reinforcement)

Key language

Cero, diez, quince, veinte, veinticinco, treinta, treinta y cinco, cuarenta, cincuenta, sesenta, setenta, ochenta, noventa, cien, ciento diez, doscientos, trescientos, cuatrocientos, quinientos, seiscientos, setecientos, ochocientos, novecientos, mil
¿Qué desea?
una botella de limonada

200 gramos de queso
500 gramos de jamón
una barra de pan
un cartón de leche
un paquete de galletas
una caja de pasteles
una lata de sardinas
¿Algo más?
Sí,…/No, nada más gracias.

Resources

Cassette A, side 2
CD 1, tracks 24, 25 and 26
Cuaderno A, page 16
Hojas de trabajo, Resource and Assessment File, pages 26 and 27 (*el queso, el pan, las galletas, un pastel*)
Flashcards 18–25

Starter 1

Aim: To practise numbers 100–1000.

Call out numbers between 100–1000 (*cien, trescientos, quinientos, etc.*).

Ask pupils to write these down on mini whiteboards or paper as you call them out and hold them up. If your class appears to be confident with these big numbers try adding some numerals (*ciento diez, doscientos treinta y tres, quinientos cincuenta y ocho etc.*).

🖾 Suggestion

Play the number game 'rubbing out'. Divide the class into two teams. Split the board in half and write 8 'big' numbers on each side (the same ones for each side). Invite a volunteer up from each team. Ask them to stand in front of the board with their backs to it and give each a whiteboard pen/piece of chalk. Call out a number. The first person to find the number you have called out and to draw a line through it gets a point for their team. Invite the next two up and so on.

Use Flashcards 18–25 to introduce quantities.

1a Escucha y escribe los números. (AT1/2)

✖ *Listening for information/instructions, Level A*

Listening. Ask pupils to listen to the recording and write down the ten numbers.

Answers

35, 40, 75, 80, 95, 100, 110, 300, 410, 500

Tapescript

treinta y cinco
cuarenta
setenta y cinco
ochenta
noventa y cinco
cien
ciento diez
trescientos
cuatrocientos diez
quinientos

1b Escribe los números. (AT1/2)

✖ *Exchange information/ideas, Level A*

Writing. Ask pupils to write out the numbers.

Answers

As tapescript for **1a**

1c Escribe diez números del 31 al 500. Lee los números a tu compañero/a. Tu compañero/a los escribe. (AT2/2)

✖ *Speaking to convey information, Level A/B*

Speaking. Working in pairs (or groups of four), pupils write down ten numbers and then read them out to their partner who writes them down.

➕ 🖾 Bingo! If you have a game in school or at home, bring this in and have a class bingo competition. A great way to practise numbers!

4 Cien gramos de jamón y una barra de pan

2a Lee la lista de la compra y empareja las cosas con los articulos en la foto. (AT3/2)

✉ *Reading for information/instructions, Level C*

Reading. Pupils match the articles on the shopping list at the bottom of page 30 with the items numbered in the picture using knowledge of language and deduction.

Answers

1 un cartón de leche	**5** una lata de sardinas
2 una caja de pasteles	**6** un paquete de galletas
3 una barra de pan	**7** 500 gramos de jamón
4 200 gramos de queso	**8** una botella de limonada

2b Escucha y comprueba tus respuestas.

✉ *Listening for information/instructions, Level B*

Listening. Pupils listen to the recording and check their answers.

Tapescript

1 un cartón de leche
2 una caja de pasteles
3 una barra de pan
4 200 gramos de queso
5 una lata de sardinas
6 un paquete de galletas
7 500 gramos de jamón
8 una botella de limonada

2c Mira la foto en **2a** otra vez y escucha las conversaciones en la tienda de comestibles. ¿Qué desean los clientes? (1–5) (AT1/4) [8L1, 3]

✉ *Listening for information/instructions, Level D*

Listening. Pupils listen to the recording and look at the photo. Ask them to write down what each customer wants. The first one is done for them.

Answers

1 5, 3, 1   **2** 6, 8   **3** 7, 1   **4** 3, 8   **5** 4, 1

You could follow this up with a second listening and draw pupils' attention to colloquial phrases – for example *¿Qué desea?*, *¿Algo mas?*, *Nada más, gracias*, etc.

Tapescript

1 – *¿Qué desea?*
  – *Una lata de sardinas y dos barras de pan, por favor.*
  – *¿Algo más?*
  – *Sí, un cartón de leche.*
2 – *¿Qué desea, señora?*
  – *Dos paquetes de galletas y una botella de limonada.*
  – *Tome usted.*
3 – *Buenos días. ¿Qué desea?*
  – *200 gramos de jamón, y un cartón de leche, por favor.*
  – *Tome usted, 200 gramos de jamón y un cartón de leche.*
4 – *Buenas tardes. ¿Qué desea señor?*
  – *Una barra de pan y una botella de limonada.*
  – *¿Algo más?*
  – *Nada más gracias.*
5 – *¡Hola!*
  – *¡Hola! Cien gramos de queso, por favor.*
  – *Vale. Aquí tiene.*
  – *Y dos cartones de leche.*
  – *¿Algo más?*
  – *No, nada más gracias.*

3 Con tu compañero/a, haz un diálogo entre un/a cliente y un/a tendero/a en la tienda de comestibles. (AT2/3–4) [8S6]

✉ *Speaking and interacting with others, Level C/D*

Speaking. Working in pairs (or groups of four), pupils pretend to buy things in a grocer's.

4 Escribe una lista de la compra para una merienda para cinco amigos. (AT4/2–3) [8T6]

✉ *Exchange information/ideas, Level A/B*

Writing. Ask pupils to write out a shopping list for a picnic with five friends.

➕ You could ask pupils to write out a 'healthy' shopping list and a 'not-so-healthy' shopping list.

En casa

Personal dossier. Get pupils to involve their families. At meal times they can try and teach them the words for food/drink items (look up any they don't know in a dictionary) and practise them. Here's the challenge! Get them to try to keep the week's shopping list in Spanish including quantities, and then if at all possible go on the shopping trip and follow the list.

4 Cien gramos de jamón y una barra de pan

Plenary

Big numbers in Spanish sound fast, long and a bit scary. Ask pupils what strategies they use to help them work these numbers out and understand them. Do they notice a pattern? Ask a couple of volunteers to explain.

Cuaderno A, page 16

1 Escribe los números apropiados. (AT3/2)

✉ *Reading for information/instructions, Level B*

Reading. Pupils fill in the gaps for 1–10 with appropriate numbers from the box.

Answers

1 42	**2** 85	**3** 59	**4** 94	**5** 200	**6** 500	**7** 360
8 700	**9** 171	**10** 903				

2 Empareja los números. (AT3/2)

✉ *Reading for information/instructions, Level B*

Reading. Pupils match the numerals in 1–10 with the appropriate numbers from the list.

Answers

1 setenta y dos
2 sesenta y ocho
3 cuarenta y cinco
4 ciento veintitrés
5 quinientos noventa y uno
6 setecientos ochenta y cuatro
7 novecientos veintisiete
8 ochocientos nueve
9 seiscientos treinta y seis
10 cuatrocientos cincuenta

3 Empareja los nombres con los dibujos. (AT3/2)

✉ *Reading for information/instructions, Level B*

Reading. Pupils match the words a–h with the pictures 1–8.

Answers

a 2	**b** 7	**c** 3	**d** 4	**e** 8	**f** 5	**g** 1	**h** 6

Hojas de trabajo, Resource and Assessment File, pages 26 and 27

Cards for pairwork featuring various foods: pupils match the pictures to the correct words.

5 ¡Que aproveche!

(Pupil's Book pages 32–33)

Main topics

- Saying that you are hungry and thirsty
- Ordering from a menu

Key Framework objectives

- Colloquialisms 8C5 (Launch)
- Negative forms and words 8S5 (Reinforcement)

Other aims

- Pronunciation practice ('*j*', '*ll*', '*c*')

Grammar

- *Tener: tengo hambre, tengo sed*

Key language

¿Qué va(n) a tomar?
¿Qué va(n) a beber?
Para mí …/Para él …/Para ella …
gambas

patatas bravas　　*naranjada*
calamares　　　　*agua con gas*
tortilla española　*agua sin gas*
jamón serrano　　*cerveza*
chorizo　　　　　*helado de vainilla/fresa/chocolate*
aceitunas　　　　*flan*
¿Va(n) a tomar algo mas? No, nada más.

Resources

Cassette A, side 2
CD 1, tracks 27, 28 and 29
Cuaderno A, page 17
Starter 1, Resource and Assessment File, page 25
OHTs 11 and 12
Flashcards 5, 10, 11 and 17 and 19, 20 (*¡Listos! 1*)

Starter 1

Aim: Revision of food. Understanding a menu.

Prepare an OHT using *Resource and Assessment File*, page 25, which gives a selection of food and drink that you would find on a menu. Ask pupils to copy the food items and write them under the appropriate course: *de primero, de segundo, de beber, de postre*. This activity provides an opportunity to practise the '*j*', '*ll*' and '*c*' (hard and soft) sounds.

Alternatively, put on OHT 11. Ask pupils to work with a partner and discuss where the food and drink should go. Invite volunteers up to write in the answers on the menu using a water soluble pen or place the food and drink from OHT 12 (first photocopy this onto a thick acetate and cut out the labels for pupils to place).

1a Lee y escucha. (AT1/4)

✂ *Knowing about language*

Reading/Listening. Ask pupils to listen to the recording and follow the conversation at the top of page 32.

Tapescript

– *¿Tienes hambre?*
– *Bueno … no tengo mucha hambre.*
– *Bueno, voy a pedir unas tapas. ¿Tienes sed?*
– *Sí, tengo sed.*
– *¿Qué vas a beber?*
– *Agua con gas.*

– *¿Qué van a tomar?*
– *Calamares, unas patatas bravas … y jamón serrano.*
– *¿Y qué van a beber?*
– *Una naranjada para mí. Y para él, agua con gas.*

– *¿Van a tomar algo más?*
– *Un helado de fresa, vainilla y chocolate.*

1b Lee y escucha el texto otra vez. ¿Verdad (✓) o mentira (✗)? (AT3/3)

✂ *Reading for information/instructions, Level D*

Listening/Reading. Pupils listen to the recording again and write down true or false for 1–5.

Answers

1 ✗　2 ✓　3 ✓　4 ✗　5 ✓

✚ Ask pupils to write down the correct answers for those that are false.

1c Mira el menú otra vez. Escucha y escribe los números de las cosas mencionadas (1–6) (AT1/3) [8L1, 3; 8C5]

✂ *Listening for information/instructions, Level D*

Listening. Pupils listen to the recording and write down the names of the things mentioned. You could then play the recording again and draw pupils' attention to some useful phrases.

Answers

1 1, 3	**2** 11, 9	**3** 7, 8	**4** 1, 4	**5** 8, 10	**6** 12, 13

Tapescript

1 – *Hola. ¿Qué va a tomar?*
– *Gambas y calamares, por favor.*
2 – *¿Qué van a beber?*
– *Para mí, una cerveza.*
– *Y para mí, un agua con gas.*
3 – *¿Qué va a tomar?*
– *No tengo mucha hambre. Unas aceitunas y una naranjada.*
4 – *Bueno, de tapas tenemos gambas, tortilla española y ...*
– *Tortilla española. ¡Qué bien! Tortilla para mí.*
– *Y para mí, gambas.*
5 – *¿Qué van a beber?*
– *Para mí una naranjada.*
– *Para mí agua sin gas.*
6 – *¿Qué hay de postre?*
– *Hay helado y flan.*
– *Un flan, para mí.*
– *Nada para mí.*

Starter 2 [8W5]

Aim: Expressions with '*tener*'.

Ask pupils to work with a partner. How many expressions can they think of that take '*tener*'? Get them to write these down and take feedback. Alternatively, ask a brave volunteer to stand up and act one out. The rest of the class have to try and guess.

Example: *tengo hambre, tengo sed, tengo calor, tengo frío, tengo 14 años, etc.*

2 Con tu compañero/a, haz un diálogo. (AT2/3–4) [8S6]

Speaking and interacting with others, Level C/D

Speaking. Working with a partner, pupils act out the restaurant dialogue.

3 Lee los textos. Elige dos cosas del menú para cada persona. (AT3/2) [8S5; 8W5; 9W5]

Reading for information/instructions, Level C

Reading. Pupils read 1–6 and then choose something suitable for each person to eat from the menu.

ICT activity

Get pupils to use a desktop publishing package to design a menu. They could work in pairs. Invent a name for the restaurant and have a competition to see who designs the best and tastiest menu! Another class/teacher could judge the menus.

Plenary

Quick fire questions. Ask pupils how to say: I'm hungry, I'm thirsty, for me ..., for her ...

Cuaderno A, page 17

1 Mira los dibujos y descifra los anagramas. (AT4/1)

Exchange information/ideas, Level A

Reading. Pupils work out the anagrams for 1–7.

Answers

1 aceitunas **2** naranjada **3** patatas bravas **4** flan
5 tortilla española **6** cerveza **7** agua mineral

2 Completa el diálogo para ti empleando las palabras en **1**. (AT3/2, 4/2–3)

Writing imaginatively, Level C

Reading and writing. Pupils complete the dialogue with their own information using words from activity 1 to help them.

Answers (*example*)

Para mí, calamares.
Patatas bravas, por favor.
De postre tomo un flan.
Y para beber, una cerveza, por favor.

6 La comida sana

(Pupil's Book pages 34–35)

Main topics

- Talking about healthy eating

Key Framework objectives

- Language and text types 8T3 (Reinforcement)
- Verb tenses (present) 8W5 (Reinforcement)
- Negative forms and words 8S5 (Reinforcement)

Grammar

- The imperative: *come, bebe*
- Talking about frequency: *al, a la*

Key language

Come (fruta) …
Bebe (leche) …
algunas veces al mes
algunas veces a la semana
todos los días

Resources

Cassette A, side 2
CD 1, track 30
Cuaderno A, page 18

Starter 1 [8W5]

Aim: revision of regular –er verbs: *comer* and *beber*

Before your class comes in write the following paradigm on the board, or prepare an OHT.

Yo com…, tu com…, él com…, (nosotros com…, vosotros com…, ellos com…) Do this second part of the paradigm depending on ability of class.

Ask pupils to fill in the endings. When they have done this and you have gone over them write out the paradigm for *beber*, if time allows.

Suggestion

Brainstorm. Find out from your class what 'healthy eating' means to them. Ask them to make a list of foods in Spanish that are healthy and unhealthy, using a dictionary to help them.

Before tackling the questions help pupils to familiarise themselves with the text. Write up a list of English words and ask pupils to find the Spanish from the text. The items are cognates or near cognates. For example; diet, tradition, mediterranean, inhabitants, United States, problems, region, includes. You could use this as an alternative to Starter 1.

1 Lee la información. ¿Verdad (3) o mentira (7)? (AT3/4) [8T3]

✖ *Reading for information/instructions, Level E*

Reading. Pupils look at the information about healthy eating at the top of page 34 and write down true or false for 1–6.

Answers

1 ✓ 2 ✗ 3 ✓ 4 ✗ 5 ✓ 6 ✓

➕ Ask pupils to correct the answers that are false.

2 Escucha las entrevistas. Copia y completa el cuadro. (1–3) (AT1/3) [8S5; 8L3]

✖ *Listening for information/instructions, Level D*

Listening. Pupils copy the grid and then listen to the recording. Ask them to fill in the grid. The first one is done for them.

Answers

	carne	fruta	pan	leche
1	no	sí	sí	sí
2	sí	no	sí	sí
3	no	sí	sí	sí

Tapescript

1 – ¿Comes carne todos los días?
– No, no todos los días.
– ¿Comes fruta todos los días?
– Sí, todos los días. ¡Me encanta la fruta!
– ¿Comes pan todos los días?
– Sí.
– ¿Bebes leche todos los días?
– Sí, bebo leche todos los días.

2 – ¿Comes carne todos los días?
– Sí, sí, todos los días.
– ¿Comes fruta todos los días?
– No, no todos los días.
– ¿Comes pan todos los días?
– Sí, como pan todos los días.
– ¿Bebes leche?
– Sí, bebo leche todos los días.

3 – ¿Comes carne todos los días?
– No. ¡Soy vegetariana! No como carne.
– ¿Te gusta la fruta?
– Sí. Me gusta la fruta. Como fruta todos los días.
– ¿Comes pan todos los días?
– Sí, todos los días.
– ¿Bebes leche?
– Sí, todos los días.

3 Con tu compañero/a, haz preguntas sobre la dieta y escribe las respuestas. (AT2/3) [8S4]

✉ *Speaking and interacting with others, Level C/D*

Speaking. Working in pairs, pupils find out what sort of food their partner eats every day and write down the answers.

🖰 ICT activity

➕ You could turn this into a class survey and enter the results on a tally chart – using MS Excel enter these results in the chart wizard. Print out a bar chart and see which foods are eaten most each day by the majority of pupils and which foods the least.

4a Mira este cartel para una dieta sana. ¿Qué más debes beber y comer? (AT3/2) [8T6]

✉ *Reading for information/instructions, Level B*

Reading. Pupils look at the poster on page 35 as a start point and write down what other foods and drinks you should consume to stay healthy.

4b Diseña un póster para una dieta. Puede ser una dieta muy buena y sana o una dieta terrible. (AT4/2–4) [8T6]

✉ *Writing imaginatively, Level B–D*

Writing. Ask pupils to design a poster for a healthy or an unhealthy diet.

🖰 ICT activity

Pupils work with a partner to design this poster on the computer using software such as MS Publisher or a desktop publishing package. Tip: get them to do a design in rough first. They should discuss pictures to be used, a suitable font and the layout before doing the final design on the computer.

Cuaderno A, page 18

1a Lee los textos. ¿Con qué frecuencia comen las personas los alimentos mencionados? (AT3/3) [8S2, 5]

✉ *Reading for information/instructions, Level D*

Reading. Pupils look at the two speech bubbles for Ramón and Patricia and fill in the grid with information about how often they eat certain foods. There is a box for pupils to look at with ticks and crosses showing different periods of time. Pupils use these to fill in the grid.

Answers

Ramón	✗	✗	✓✓	✓✓✓	✓✓
Patricia	✓✓✓	✗	✓✓		✓✓✓

1b Contesta a las preguntas. (AT3/3) [8S2, 5]

✉ *Reading for information/instructions, Level D*

Reading. Pupils answer questions 1–8 in reference to Ramón's and Patricia's eating habits.

Answers

1 Patricia **2** Ramón (Patricia) **3** Patricia
4 A few times a week **5** Every day **6** (pupil's own opinion)
7 (pupil's own opinion)

1c Escribe unas frases para describir la dieta de Susana. (AT4/2–3) [8L4]

✉ *Exchange information/ideas, Level C/D*

Writing. Pupils write a few sentences to describe Susana's diet. They will find the information about Susana's eating habits on the grid.

Answers (*example*)

Susana come queso y yogur algunas veces al mes, come pollo y pescado algunas veces a la semana y come verduras, fruta, arroz y pan todos los días.

Resumen

This is a checklist of language covered in Module 2. There is a comprehensive *Resumen* list for Module 2 in the Student's Book (page 36 and a *Resumen* test sheet in Cuaderno A (page 23)

Key Framework objectives

● Relaying gist and detail 8L3 (Reinforcement)

Prepárate

A revision test to give practice for the test itself at the end of the module.

Resources

Cassette A, side 2
CD 1, tracks 31 and 32
Cuaderno A, pages 19, 20, 21 and 22
Skills, Resource and Assessment File, page 29
Resumen, Resource and Assessment File, page 30

1a Escucha y escribe el orden en que se mencionan las frutas y verduras. (1–6) (AT1/3) [8L3]

✖ *Listening for information/instructions, Level D*

Listening. Pupils listen to the recording and write down the order in which the fruit and vegetables are mentioned.

Answers

1 b   2 d   3 f   4 e   5 c   6 a

Tapescript

1 *¿Tiene tomates?*
2 *¿Cuánto es un kilo de uvas?*
3 *Me gustan los plátanos.*
4 *Las lechugas están a dos euros.*
5 *Deme un kilo de patatas.*
6 *Medio kilo de peras, por favor.*

1b Escucha la conversación y contesta a las preguntas. (AT1/4) [8L3]

✖ *Listening for information/instructions, Level D*

Listening. Pupils listen to the conversation and write down the answers for 1–3 in English.

Answers

1 onions, oranges   **2** $\frac{1}{2}$kg onions, $1\frac{1}{2}$ oranges   **3** 3,50 euros

Tapescript

– *Buenos días.*
– *Buenos días. ¿Qué desea?*
– *Medio kilo de cebollas, por favor.*
– *¿Algo más?*
– *Kilo y medio de naranjas.*
– *Aquí tiene.*
– *¿Cuánto es en total?*
– *Son 3 euros 50.*
– *Tome usted.*
– *Gracias.*
– *De nada. Adiós.*

2 Mira el menú y los dibujos. Con tu compañero/a, haz un diálogo entre un/a camarero/a y un/a cliente. (AT2/3–4)

✖ *Speaking and interacting with others, Level C/D*

Speaking. Role-play.

3a Lee la carta. ¿Verdad (✓) o mentira (✗)? (AT3/4)

✖ *Reading for information/instructions, Level D*

Reading. True or false.

Answers

1 ✗   2 ✗   3 ✓   4 ✗   5 ✗   6 ✓   7 ✗   8 ✗

3b Lee la carta en **3a** otra vez y escribe una similar para ti. (AT4/3–4) [8T6]

✖ *Exchange information/ideas, Level C/D*

Writing. Pupils write a similar letter to that in **3a**.

Cuaderno A, page 19

Repaso 1

1 Mira el anuncio del supermercado y contesta a las preguntas. (AT3/2) [8T3]

✖ *Reading for information/instructions, Level B*

Reading. Pupils look at the supermarket advert and answer questions 1–8. You will need to teach *los melocotones* (peaches)

Answers

1 1,45€   **2** 2,69€   **3** 1,08€   **4** 0,89€   **5** 0,83€
6 0,91€   **7** 0,53€   **8** 0,72€

2 Diseña un folleto de tus productos favoritos con precios. Busca las palabras que no conoces en el diccionario. (AT4/1–3) [8T3, 6; 9T5]

✉ *Writing imaginatively, Level B/C*

Writing. Pupils design a leaflet to advertise their favourite products, with prices. Remind them to look up words they don't know in the dictionary.

Cuaderno A, page 20

Repaso 2

1a Mira el menú y rellena el cuadro. (AT3/3) [8T3]

✉ *Reading for information/instructions, Level C*

Reading. Pupils look at the menu and fill in the grid.

Answers

Milkshake flavours	chocolate vanilla strawberry yoghurt
Juices	tomato pineapple peach
Other drinks	hot chocolate beer milk
Types of cake	chocolate cheese home made white chocolate
Sandwich fillings	chorizo, salmon, blue cheese, peppers, plain cheese
Other snacks	croissant, tortilla

1b Mira el menú otra vez y contesta a las preguntas. (AT3/3) [8T3]

✉ *Reading for information/instructions, Level C*

Reading. Pupils use the menu to answer questions 1–4.

Answers

1 3,61€   **2** 3,91€   **3** 1,95€   **4** 2,25€

1c Elige del menú y completa las frases. (AT4/2–3) [8T3]

✉ *Exchange information/ideas, Level C*

Reading and writing. Pupils choose items from the menu for themselves, friends and family to eat and drink.

Cuaderno A, page 21

Gramática 1

1 Write your opinion of these dishes. [8W4]

✉ *Knowing about language*

Reading and writing. Pupils use the vocabulary in the boxes to write their opinion about dishes 1–8.

2 What do you think of these dishes and products? Choose words from the box to complete the sentences. [8W4]

✉ *Knowing about language*

Reading. Pupils choose appropriate adjectives from the boxes to describe their opinions of the dishes/products in 1–8.

Cuaderno A, page 22

Gramática 2

1 Mira los calendarios y elige la frase apropiada para cada uno.

✉ *Knowing about language*

Reading. Pupils look at the calendars and choose the appropriate time phrase from the box for each one.

Answers

1 una vez al año   **2** una vez al mes
3 una vez a la semana   **4** dos veces a la semana
5 tres veces a la semana

Skills, Resource and Assessment File, page 29 (Pronunciation and spelling)

1a
Answers

3

1b
Answers

4

2

Answers

a 3	b 2	c 1	d 2	e 4	f 4
g 3	h 4	i 3	j 2		

3a

Answers

They all contain *vowels*.

3b

Answers

a patatas
b fruta
c pan
d agua
e hamburguesas
f ensalada
g pescado
h naranjada
i verduras
j queso

4

Answers

a pescado
b comida
c desayuno
d lechuga
e pollo
f sopa
g helado

5

Answers

a ver du ras
b sar di nas
c chul et as
d en sal ad a
e pa ell a
f nar an jas
g ce boll as
h tom at es
i que so
j cho ri zo

6

Answers

Pupils' anagrams.

7 ¡Extra! ¡Feliz Navidad!

(Pupil's Book pages 38–39)

This is an optional unit which revises and extends some of the key language of the module: It looks at how Christmas and New Year are celebrated in Spain.

Key Framework objectives

● Question types 8S4 (Reinforcement)
● Language and text types 8T3 (Reinforcement)

● Dictionary use 8T4 (Reinforcement)
● Poems/jokes/songs 8C4 (Launch)

Resources

Cassette A, side 2
CD 1, tracks 33 and 34

Starter 1 [8T4]

Aim: Glossary/Dictionary practice.

Ask pupils to look up the meaning of the following words in the glossary. Do this before directing pupils to the unit.

canción, adornar, cantar, mandar, pavo, regalo, belén

1 Lee el texto y contesta a las preguntas. (AT3/4) [8T3]

✄ *Reading for information/instructions, Level E*

Reading. Ask pupils to read *¿Cómo se celebra la Navidad en España?*. Answer questions 1–6 in English.

Answers

1 24th December	**4** midnight
2 Christmas Eve	**5** 6th January
3 fish and nougat	**6** 12 grapes

2 ¿Cómo se celebra la Navidad en el Reino Unido? Escucha la conversación y completa las frases con las palabras apropiadas. (1–7) (AT1/4) [8L3]

✄ *Listening for information/instructions, Level D*

Listening. Pupils listen to the recording and do the multiple choice for 1–7.

Answers

1 a **2** b **3** a **4** a **5** b **6** b **7** a

Tapescript

1 – ¿Cómo celebras la Navidad en el Reino Unido? ¿Qué celebras más, Nochebuena o el Día de Navidad?
 – Celebro más el veinticinco de diciembre.
2 – ¿Adornas un árbol?
 – Sí, adorno un árbol con luces.
3 – ¿Cantas villancicos?
 – Sí, muchos como 'Silent Night'.
4 – ¿Mandas tarjetas?

 – Sí, mando muchas tarjetas.
5 – ¿Cuándo recibes los regalos?
 – Recibo los regalos el Día de Navidad.
6 – ¿Cenas algo especial el Día de Navidad?
 – No, el Día de Navidad como una comida especial en casa con la familia.
7 – ¿Qué comes el Día de Navidad?
 – Como pavo.

Starter 2

Aim: Vocabulary revision.

Brainstorm words that are useful when talking about festivals. To make the vocabulary revision easier an alternative would be to put up some key words for pupils to match to the English.

3a Con tu compañero/a, elige una fiesta. Contesta y pregunta. (AT2/4)

✄ *Speaking and interacting with others, Level D/E*

Speaking. Working in pairs, pupils take it in turns to ask about festivals celebrated in their partner's house.

3b ¿Qué fiesta celebras más en tu casa? Contesta a las preguntas. (AT4/3–4) [8S4]

✄ *Exchange information/ideas, Level C–E*

Writing. Pupils answer the questions and write about a festival they celebrate at home.

✏ ICT activity

Using a design package such as MS Publisher ask pupils to design a card to celebrate an important festival (Diwali, Christmas, Hannukah, etc.) with appropriate wording in Spanish.

Plenary

Ask pupils to work in pairs. Discuss and write down two strategies they use to help them read long texts in Spanish. Take feedback.

7 ¡Extra! ¡Feliz Navidad!

Escucha y lee la canción y busca las palabras que no conoces en el diccionario. [8C4]

✉ *Listening for enjoyment*

Listening: Pupils listen to the song and look up any unfamiliar words in the dictionary.

Tapescript

Un villancico

Campana sobre campana
y sobre campana una,
asómate a la ventana
verás al Niño en la cuna.

Belén, campanas de Belén,
que los ángeles tocan
¿qué nuevas me traéis?

Recogido tu rebaño
¿adónde vas pastorcillo?
Voy a llevar al portal
requesón, manteca y vino.

Belén, campanas de Belén,
que los ángeles tocan
¿qué nuevas me traéis?

Campana sobre campana
y sobre campana dos,
asómate a la ventana
porque está naciendo Dios.

Belén, campanas de Belén,
que los ángeles tocan
¿qué nuevas me traéis?

Aprende y canta el villancico.

Reading: Pupils can then learn the song and sing it together!

Te toca a ti
(Pupil's Book pages 110–111)

- Self-access reading and writing at two levels

Key Framework objectives

- Negative forms and words 8S5 (Reinforcement)
- Coloquialisms 8C5 (Reinforcement)

A Reinforcement

1 Empareja la comida con los dibujos. (AT3/1)

✉ *Reading for information/instructions, Level A*

Reading. Pupils match the food (1–11) with the drawings (a–k)

Answers

1 c	2 a	3 j	4 k	5 f	6 i	7 b	8 g	9 e	10 d	11 h

2 Copia y completa el cuadro. (AT3/2) [8S5]

✉ *Reading for information/instructions, Level C*

Reading. Pupils copy out and fill in the grid with information from the three letters: likes and dislikes.

Answers

	Le encanta (m)	Le gusta (m)	No le gusta (m)	Odia
Eduardo	chuletas	gambas	perritos calientes	sardinas
Carmina	helado	verduras	ensalada	flan
Jaime	fruta	patatas	verduras	cebollas

3 ¿Qué opinas de la comida? Escribe cuatro listas. (AT4/2) [8S5]

✉ *Exchange information/ideas, Level A*

Writing. Pupils make four lists of food they like/dislike: *me encanta(n), me gusta(n), no me gusta(n), odio*

B Extension

1a Empareja los números. (AT3/2)

✉ *Reading for information/instructions, Level B*

Reading. Pupils match the numbers.

Answers

1 h	2 a	3 e	4 g	5 d	6 f	7 c	8 b

1b Escribe los números en palabras. (AT4/2)

✉ *Knowing about language*

Writing. Pupils write out the numbers in words.

Answers

a trescientos setenta y siete   **b** quinientos setenta y nueve
c ciento catorce   **d** setecientos veintiséis
e doscientos cuarenta y seis   **f** ochocientos noventa y uno

2 Pon las frases de la conversación en el orden correcto. (AT3/3) [8C5]

✉ *Reading for information/instructions, Level D*

Reading. Pupils put the conversation in the correct order.

Answers

1 e	2 d	3 c	4 g	5 b	6 a	7 f

3 Mira el cuadro y escribe seis frases sobre la comida. (AT4/3) [8S5]

✉ *Exchange information/ideas, Level C/D*

Writing. Pupils use the writing frame to write six sentences about food.

De compras

(Pupil's Book pages 42–59)

Unit	Key Framework objectives	PoS	Key language and Grammar
1 ¿Qué ropa llevan? (pp. 42–43) Talking about clothes Comparing prices	8S1 Word, phrase and clause sequencing [L] 8W1 Adding abstract words [R] 8T4 Dictionary use [R]	3d use reference materials 4a working with authentic materials	Comparatives: *más* + adjective + *que* Adjectives: *barato/a(s), caro/a(s), grande(s), pequeño/a(s)* *Lleva una camiseta, un jersey, …*
2 Me gusta aquella camiseta roja (pp. 44–45) Talking about clothes you like Talking about clothes you dislike	8T7 Inflections and word order [L] 8W4 Word endings [R] 8S1 Word, phrase and clause sequencing [R]	5c express opinions	Demonstrative adjectives: *Este, esta, estos, estas* *Ese, esa, esos, esas* *Aquel, aquella, aquellos, aquellas* Adjectives of colour: *rojo, roja, rojos, rojas* *Me gusta(n) …/No me gusta(n) …* *Prefiero …* *Me encanta(n) …*
3 ¿Me lo puedo probar? (pp. 46–47) Shopping for clothes	8W4 Word endings [R] 8T7 Inflections and word order [R] 8L1 Listening for subtleties [R]	2a listen for gist and detail 5c express opinions	Direct object pronouns: *lo, la, los, las* Demonstrative adjectives: *Este, esta, estos, estas* *Ese, esa, esos, esas* *Me gusta este jersey ¿Me lo puedo probar?* *Me gustan estas botas ¿Me las puedo probar?* *¿Qué número lleva Ud?* *¿Qué talla lleva Ud?*
4 ¿Qué vas a llevar para ir a la fiesta? (pp. 48–49) Describing clothing Asking about clothes Saying what you are going to wear	8W5 Verbs (near future) [L] 8S7 Present, past, *future* [L]	2a listen for gist and detail 5e range of resources	The immediate future: *ir + a* + infinitive *¿Qué vas a llevar para ir a la fiesta?* *Voy a llevar pantalones negros y un top rosa.* *Voy a llevar unos zapatos blancos.*
5 ¿Llevas uniforme? (pp. 32–33) Talking about your school uniform Colours	8S2 Connectives [L] 8T6 Text as model and source [L] 8W4 Word endings [R] 8C3 Daily life/young people	4c compare cultures 4d consider experiences in other countries 5c express opinions 5e range of resources	Adjectives of colour: *azules, …* Comparisons: *más, menos* *El uniforme escolar: una chaqueta negra, una falda roja, …* *Es más/menos (elegante).*
6 En la calle principal (pp. 52–53) Talking about types of shops Saying where you can buy things	8S3 Modal verbs [L] 8W5 Verbs (near future) [R]	1a sounds and writing 3a memorising 3c use knowledge of English	Present tense of *poder: puedo, puedes* *¿Dónde puedo comprar (pan)?* *Puedo/puedes comprar (pan) en (la panadería).*

Unit	Key Framework objectives	PoS	Key language and Grammar
Resumen y Prepárate (pp. 54–55) Pupil's checklist and practice test	8W5 Verbs (near future) [R]		
7 ¡Extra! ¿Cuál es tu estilo? (pp. 56–57) Optional unit: Style test	8W7 Dictionary detail [L] 9C3 Youth attitudes to sport/popular culture [L] 9T3 Authentic text as sources [R]	3b use context to interpret meaning 4a working with authentic materials 5d respond to different types of language	
Te toca a ti (pp. 112–113) Self-access reading and writing at two levels			

1 ¿Qué ropa llevan?
(Pupil's Book pages 42–43)

Main Topics

- Talking about clothes
- Comparing prices

Key Framework objectives

- Word, phrase and clause sequencing 8S1 (Launch)
- Adding abstract words 8W1 (Reinforcement)
- Dictionary use 8T4 (Reinforcement)

Grammar

- Comparatives: *más* + adjective + *que*
- Adjectives: *barato, caro, grande, pequeño*

Key language

Lleva …
una camisa   unos zapatos

una blusa   una camiseta
una falda   unos vaqueros
unas botas   unos calcetines
una chaqueta   unos pantalones
un jersey

Resources

Cassette B, side 1
CD 2, tracks 2 and 3
Cuaderno A, page 24
Starter 1, Resource and Assessment File, page 45
Hojas de trabajo, Resource and Assessment File, pages 48 and 49 (*la camisa, la falda, las botas, el jersey, los pantalones, los zapatos, los vaqueros, los calcetines, la chaqueta, las zapatillas de deporte*)
OHTs 13, 14

Starter 1 [8S1]

Aim: Revision of Comparatives.

Text manipulation (jumbled up sentences): Prepare an OHT of the following sentences using *Resource and Assessment File*, page 45. Ask pupils to un-jumble them. See who can finish first.

1 el más La Torre Eiffel que alta Big Ben es
   (*La Torre Eiffel es más alta que el Big Ben*)

2 *La es nutritiva que los perritos calientes paella más* (*La paella es más nutritiva que los perritos calientes*)

3 *es deporte El más que interesante la geografía* (*El deporte/La geografía es más interesante que la geografía/el deporte*)

Suggestion

Bring in a bag of clothes (could be fancy dress!) and introduce them by putting them on, or ask for a volunteer or volunteers to put the clothes on as you introduce them. Name the clothes and ask your class to repeat them with you.

1 Escucha y escribe el orden en que se mencionan los artículos. (1–11) (AT3/1)

✉ *Listening for information/instructions, Level A*

Listening. Pupils listen to the recording and write down the order in which the articles of clothing are mentioned.

Answers

1 c	2 b	3 e	4 j	5 a	6 h	7 g	8 k	9 d	10 i	11 f

Tapescript

1 *una falda*
2 *una blusa*
3 *unos pantalones*
4 *un jersey*
5 *una camisa*
6 *unos vaqueros*
7 *una camiseta*
8 *una chaqueta*
9 *unas botas*
10 *unos calcetines*
11 *unos zapatos*

2a Mira los dibujos y escucha. ¿Verdad (✓) o mentira (✗)? (1–10) (AT1/2) [8L3]

✉ *Listening for information/instructions, Level B*

Listening/Reading. Pupils look at drawings 1–3 and listen to the recording. Ask pupils to write down true (✓) or false (✗) for 1–10.

Answers

1 ✓	2 ✓	3 ✗	4 ✗	5 ✓	6 ✓	7 ✗	8 ✓	9 ✗	10 ✓

Tapescript

1 *Ester lleva una blusa.*
2 *Martín lleva una camisa.*
3 *Ester lleva unos pantalones.*
4 *Isabel lleva un jersey.*
5 *Martín lleva zapatos y calcetines.*
6 *Isabel lleva una chaqueta.*
7 *Martín lleva una falda.*
8 *Isabel lleva una camiseta.*
9 *Ester lleva zapatos.*
10 *Isabel lleva vaqueros y zapatillas.*

2b Describe lo que llevan Ester, Martín e Isabel. Tu compañero/a dice verdad o mentira. (AT2/2–3)

✠ *Speaking and interacting with others, Level C*

Speaking. Working in pairs, pupils describe what each person is wearing. Their partner answers true or false.

▣ *Fui al Corte Inglés y compré …*

Pupils sit in a circle and say the above sentence adding an item of clothing. The next must say their own item of clothing in addition to those mentioned previously. If they can't remember then they are out. You could make this more difficult by passing round a bag of clothes or a box with pictures of single items of clothing. The pupil must pick an item from the bag, say what it is and also name all items previously pulled from the bag.

✚ Ask pupils to write down what they normally wear on a Saturday and illustrate. e.g.: *Llevo vaqueros y un jersey.*

Starter 2

Aim: Revise regular *–ar* verbs.

Choose an *–ar* verb: *llevar, hablar, comprar,* etc. Use a dice where dots correspond to each subject pronoun, e.g. one dot = *yo*, two dots = *tú*, three dots = *él*, etc. or dice with subject pronouns on them. Pupils work with a partner or a small group and conjugate the verb according to the dot or the subject pronoun it lands on. Or you could practise *llevar* in more depth. Ask pupils to throw the dice and then, depending on the subject pronoun or number of dots it lands on, they must say what the person is wearing. Example: *Llevo uniforme escolar, llevas una camiseta blanca y pantalones negros,* etc.

3 Mira el catálogo. Busca las palabras que no conoces en el diccionario. (AT3/4) [8T4]

✠ *Reading for information/instructions, Level D*

Reading. Pupils look at the catalogue extract and look up the words they don't know in the dictionary.

4 Empareja las dos partes correctas de las frases. (AT3/4) [8W1]

✠ *Knowing about language*

Reading. Pupils match the sentences (1–8) with their other halves (a–h).

Answers

1 c 2 a 3 d 4 b 5 f 6 e 7 h 8 g

5 Escribe una lista de ropa que te gustaría comprar del catálogo. (AT4/1–2)

✠ *Exchange information/ideas, Level B*

Writing. Pupils write out a list of clothes they would like to buy from the catalogue.

✚ Bring in real Spanish clothing catalogues or pictures taken from authentic material. Ask pupils to work with a partner and choose clothes they like and get them to write down five of them.

Plenary

Ask a brave person or persons to explain how they matched the sentence halves in activity 4 (e.g. looking at context, choosing the correct form of *ser*, finding suitable matches with adjectives, etc.).

Cuaderno A, page 24

1a Empareja las descripciones con las personas. (AT3/2)

✠ *Reading for information/instructions, Level B*

Reading. Pupils match the descriptions (a–c) with the pictures (1–3).

Answers

1 c 2 a 3 b

1b Mira el dibujo y describe lo que lleva Carmen. (AT4/2)

✠ *Exchange information/ideas, Level C*

Writing. Pupils look at the picture and describe what Carmen is wearing.

Answers

Carmen lleva una falda, una camiseta (ajustada) y las botas.

2 Lee las frases y mira los dibujos. ¿Verdad (✓) o mentira (✗)? (AT3/2)

✠ *Reading for information/instructions, Level B*

Reading. Pupils look at the clothes pictures (1–8) and decide whether sentences 1–6 are true or false.

Answers

1 ✓ 2 ✗ 3 ✓ 4 ✓ 5 ✓ 6 ✗

Hojas de trabajo, Resource and Assessment File, pages 48 and 49

Cards for pairwork featuring items of clothing: pupils match the pictures to the correct words.

2 Me gusta aquella camiseta roja

(Pupil's Book pages 44–45)

Main Topics

- Talking about clothes you like
- Talking about clothes you dislike
- Colours

Key Framework objectives

- Word endings 8W4 (Reinforcement)
- Word, phrase and clause sequencing 8S1 (Reinforcement)
- Check inflections 8T7 (Launch)

Grammar

- Demonstrative adjectives:
  Este, esta, estos estas
  Ese, esa, esos, esas
  Aquel, aquella, aquellos, aquellas
- Adjectives of colour: *rojo, roja, rojos, rojas*

Key language

Me gusta(n) …, no me gusta(n) …
Prefiero …
Me encanta(n) …

amarillo	negro
blanco	naranja
violeta	beige
verde	marrón
azul	rojo
gris	rosa

Resources

Cassette B, side 1
CD 2, tracks 4 and 5
Cuaderno A, page 25
OHTs 15,16

Starter 1 [8W4]

Aim: To introduce the demonstrative adjectives: *este, esta, estos, estas* in another familiar context before introducing them with clothes.

Write on the board some familiar nouns (e.g. food) already met in previous units. Then tell pupils you are going to write up the four words for 'this' and 'these'. You can either show them which are masculine/feminine and singular/plural or challenge them to work this out. Ask pupils to write down the correct form of 'this' or 'these' for each noun.

1 … *flan*   2 … *plátanos*   3 … *chuletas*   4 … *pera*

How did they decide which adjectives to pair with which noun?

Suggestion

Go over clothes again. Pull clothes from the box or use pictures. Revise the names quickly with your class. *¿Qué es?* Then go over them again, this time introducing colours. Go over the colours. Hold up items of clothing and ask what colour they are. *¿Qué color es? Marrón*, etc. Now introduce the item of clothing with the colour. You could hold up several examples of red articles of clothing. Ask pupils why the same colour sounds a little bit different for different articles of clothing. e.g.: *los zapatos rojos, la falda roja*. Pull out other items from the bag and see if pupils can tell you what colour they are.

1a Escribe el color. (AT3/1)

✉ *Reading for information/instructions, Level A*

Reading. Ask pupils to write down what each colour is for a–l.

Answers

a rojo	b azul	c amarillo	d verde	e blanco	f negro
g gris	h marrón	i beige	j naranja	k violeta	l rosa

1b Escucha y comprueba tus respuestas. (AT1/1)

✉ *Listening for information/instructions, Level A*

Listening. Pupils listen to the recording and correct their answers to 1a.

Tapescript

As answers to 1a

Starter 2 [8W4]

Aim: To practise agreement of colours with nouns.

Ask pupils to work with a partner. They take it in turns to pull out something from their pencil case. Their partner says what it is and what colour it is. Remind pupils that the colour must agree with the noun. e.g.: *una goma blanca, **un lápiz negro**.* Quickly go round the class, ask pupils to hold up an item from their pencil case, say what it is and what colour it is.

2a Escucha y escribe el orden en que se menciona la ropa. (1–8) (AT1/3) [8L3]

✉ *Listening for information/instructions, Level C*

Listening. Ask pupils to listen to the recording and write down the letter of the item of clothing for 1–8.

Answers

1 b	**2** g	**3** i	**4** e	**5** k	**6** h	**7** c	**8** d

Tapescript

1 Me gusta aquella camiseta roja.
2 A mí, no. Pero me gustan esos pantalones azules.
3 Me gusta este jersey violeta.
4 Me gusta ese jersey en negro.
5 Me gustan estos zapatos marrones.
6 Yo prefiero esas zapatillas blancas.
7 Aquellos vaqueros son baratos.
8 Me gustan aquellas botas marrones.

2b Con tu compañero/a, habla de la ropa en los dibujos en **2a** que te gusta y no te gusta. (AT2/2–3) [8W4; 8S1]

✄ *Experiences, feelings, opinions, Level C/D*

Speaking. Working in pairs, pupils look at the clothes in the picture at the bottom of page 44. They say which clothes they like (including the colour) and which they dislike.

2c Completa las frases con la forma apropiada de *aquel, este* o *ese*. [8W4]

✄ *Knowing about language*

Reading. Pupils fill in the gaps with the appropriate demonstrative adjective for 1–8.

Answers

1 aquella **2** ese **3** aquella **4** este **5** esas
6 estos **7** aquellos **8** esta

➕ Ask pupils to justify their answers. e.g.: **1** *camiseta* is feminine singular so it is *aquella*.

3 Elige cinco cosas de **2a** y escribe frases. (AT4/3) [8W4; 8S1; 8T7]

✄ *Exchange information/ideas, Level C/D*

Writing. Ask pupils to choose five items of clothing from **2a** and to write sentences explaining why they like/dislike them.

ICT activity

Ask pupils to wordprocess activities **2c** and **3**.

Plenary [8W4]

Ask pupils how to say: this, that, these, those (no peeping in books!)

Can someone explain the subtle difference between *aquel* and *ese* (*aquel* is used for things furthest away)?

How do adjectives of colour work? Give examples.

Cuaderno A, page 25

1 Elige la forma apropiada del adjetivo. [8W4]

✄ *Knowing about language*

Reading. Pupils choose the correct colour adjective to describe each item of clothing for sentences 1–6.

Answers

1 negros **2** azul **3** amarillo **4** roja **5** marrones
6 blanca

2 Empareja las frases. (AT3/2)

✄ *Reading for information/instructions, Level C*

Reading. Pupils match the sentences.

Answers

1 e **2** c **3** f **4** a **5** b **6** d

3 Mira los dibujos y elige la palabra correcta en cada caso.

✄ *Knowing about language*

Reading. Pupils look at the pictures to help them choose the correct demonstrative adjective for each sentence (1–6).

Answers

1 esta **2** ese **3** aquellas **4** esas **5** Ese **6** Esta

3 ¿Me lo puedo probar?
(Pupil's Book pages 46–47)

Main topics
- Shopping for clothes
- Asking if you can try them on
- Asking how much they cost

Key Framework objectives
- Word endings 8W4 (Reinforcement)
- Checking inflections 8T7 (Reinforcement)
- Listening for subtleties 8L1

Grammar
- Direct object pronouns:
  lo, la, los, las
- Demonstrative adjectives:
  este, esta, estos, estas
  ese, esa, esos, esas

Key language
Me gusta este jersey ¿Me lo puedo probar?
Me gusta esta falda. ¿Me la puedo probar?
Me gustan estas botas ¿Me las puedo probar?
Me gustan estos vaqueros. ¿Me los puedo probar?
¿Qué número lleva Ud?
¿Qué talla lleva Ud?

Resources
Cassette B, side 1
CD 2, tracks 6 and 7
Cuaderno A, page 26
Starter 1 and 2, Resource and Assessment File,
pages 45 and 46
OHTs 17, 18

Starter 1 [8W4]
Aim: To recap agreement of adjectives with nouns and the use of the definite article.

Use *Resource and Assessment File*, page 45 on the OHT or as a Worksheet or write the following on the board. Ask pupils to fill in the definite article and the appropriate ending to each colour.

1 *me gusta … cinturón roj…*
2 *me gustan … botas negr…*
3 *no me gusta … chaqueta naranj…*
4 *me encantan … vaqueros blanc…*

1a Empareja los dibujos con las frases. (AT3/3)

✄ *Reading for information/instructions, Level C*

Reading. Pupils match the drawings (a–f) with the speech bubbles (1–6).

Answers

1 f	2 d	3 b	4 e	5 a	6 c

1b Escucha y escribe las letras apropiadas para cada dibujo en **1a**. (1–5) (AT1/2)

✄ *Listening for information/instructions, Level C*

Listening. Ask pupils to listen to the recording and write down the letters of the appropriate drawings.

Answers

1 e	2 d	3 a	4 f	5 c

Tapescript
1 Me gusta la camiseta. ¿Me la puedo probar?
2 Me gustan las botas blancas. ¿Me las puedo probar?
3 Los vaqueros me encantan. ¿Me los puedo probar?
  Sí, sí.
4 Me gusta el cinturón.
  ¿El cinturón marron?
  Sí
5 ¡Hola!
  ¡Hola! Me gusta la falda rosa. ¿Me la puedo probar?

2 Con tu compañero/a, pregunta y contesta. (AT2/2–3) [8W4]

✄ *Speaking and interacting with others, Level C*

Speaking. Ask pupils to work in pairs and pretend to be trying on clothes in a clothes shop. e.g.: *Me gusta este jersey. ¿Me lo puedo probar?*

Starter 2 [8W4]
Aim: To recap direct object pronouns.

Use *Resource and Assessment File*, page 46 on the OHT or as a worksheet. Ask pupils to fill in the gaps with the appropriate form: *lo, la, los, las*

1 *Me gusta este cinturón. ¿Me … puedo probar?*
2 *Me gusta esta chaqueta. ¿Me … puedo probar?*
3 *Me gustan estas botas. ¿Me … puedo probar?*
4 *Me gustan estos zapatos. ¿Me … puedo probar?*

3a Escucha y completa los diálogos. (AT1/3) [8L1]

✄ *Listening for information/instructions, Level C*

Listening. Pupils listen to the recording and choose words from the bubble to fill in the gaps.(1–3)

Answers

1 cuestan **2** camiseta, 18 **3** zapatos, 42	

Tapescript

1 – ¡Hola!
 – ¡Hola! ¿Cuánto cuestan estos vaqueros?
 – Cuestan cuarenta y un euros.
 – ¿Me los puedo probar?
 – Sí, claro.
2 – ¿Tiene esa camiseta en treinta y ocho?
 – Sí, aquí tiene.
 – ¿Cuánto cuesta?
 – Cuesta dieciocho euros.
3 – ¿Me puedo probar esos zapatos?
 – Sí, claro. ¿Qué número usa usted?
 – Un 42, por favor.

3b Con tu compañero/a, mira los dibujos y haz diálogos como en **3a**. (AT2/3–4) [8S4]

✂ *Speaking and interacting with others, Level C/D*

Speaking. Working in pairs, pupils use the four pictures and make up shop dialogues like those in activity **3a**.

Suggestion

Set up a clothes shop. Get different groups of pupils (no more than six) to take it in turns to buy clothes.

3c Escribe los diálogos de **3b**. (AT4/3–4) [8S4; 8T7]

✂ *Writing imaginatively, Level D/E*

Writing. Pupils write out the dialogues they have just role-played in activity **3b**.

✎ ICT activity

➕ Divide pupils into groups of four. Using suitable software and a digital camera pupils make up a photostory about someone buying clothes in a shop. They must discuss the storyline and the portrait shots, decide who is going to direct and take the photos, and who is going to load the information into the computer (pictures and script). For further tips on how to make this activity flow smoothly liaise with the drama and IT departments.

Alternatively, ask pupils to carry out the above activity but use an artwork package such as 'paint box' to draw the pictures and type in the storyline. Then print it out.

Plenary [8W4]

How do you say 'Can I try it on?' in Spanish.

What are the four different ways of saying 'it' in Spanish? Why are there so many?

Cuaderno A, page 26

1 Empareja las frases. (AT3/2)

✂ *Knowing about language*

Reading. Pupils match the sentences.

Answers

1 d	**2** c	**3** a	**4** b

2 Elige las frases apropiadas para los globos. (AT3/2)

✂ *Reading for information/instructions, Level C*

Reading. Pupils choose appropriate sentences a–f to go each speech bubble in the comic strip.

Answers

1 b	**2** f	**3** c	**4** d	**5** e	**6** a

4 ¿Qué vas a llevar para ir a la fiesta? (Pupil's Book pages 48–49)

Main topics

- Describing clothes
- Asking about clothes
- Saying what you are wearing

Key Framework objectives

- Verb tenses (near future) 8W5 (Launch)
- Present, past, *future* 8S7(Launch)

Grammar

- The immediate future: *ir + a +* infinitive

Key language

Voy a llevar …
un abrigo	una gorra
un top	un traje
un vestido	una camisa

una corbata	una falda
una sudadera	unas zapatillas
(con capucha)	(de deporte)
unos zapatos	unos pantalones

Para ir …
a la boda	al partido de fútbol
a la discoteca	al parque
a la fiesta	

Resources

Cassette B, side 1
CD 2, tracks 8 and 9
Cuaderno A, page 27
Hojas de trabajo, Resource and Assessment File, pages 48 and 49 (*el cinturón, la corbata, la gorra, el abrigo, el traje*)
Grammar, Resource and Assessment File, page 50

Starter 1 [8W4]

Aim: Practising the indefinite article: *un, una, unos, unas.*

Write up the indefinite articles on the board. Call out a selection of vocabulary (see below) and ask pupils to give you or write on their mini white boards the correct form of a/an to go with each word.

1 *jersey*   2 *camisa*   3 *blusa*   4 *zapatos*
5 *pantalones*   6 *zapatillas de deporte*   7 *cinturón*

1a Mira las fotos y lee. ¿A quién se describe? (AT3/2)

✕ *Reading for information/instructions, Level C*

Reading. Pupils look at the photos at the top of page 48 and write down who is being described in 1–4.

Answers

1 Will Smith   **2** Kylie Minogue   **3** Eminem   **4** Christina Aguilera

1b Escucha y comprueba tus respuestas.

Listening. Pupils listen to the recording and check their answers.

Tapescript

1 *Will Smith lleva un traje gris y una corbata. Lleva una camisa negra.*
2 *Kylie Minogue lleva un vestido elegante y zapatos de tacón alto.*
3 *Eminem lleva una gorra, una sudadera y unos pantalones anchos.*
4 *Christina Aguilera lleva un top de lycra y una falda corta y ajustada. También lleva un abrigo estampado de leopardo.*

2 Describe a una persona de las fotos. Tu compañero/a dice quién es. (AT2/2–3)

✕ *Speaking to convey information, Level C/D*

Speaking. Working in pairs, pupils take it in turns to describe one of the people in the photos. Partners must try and guess who this person is.

Starter 2

Aim: To practise the irregular verb 'ir' (to go).

Write the following on the board and get pupils to match them up.

I am going	ella va
You are going	yo voy
She is going	tú vas
He is going	ellos van
They are going	él va

3 ¿Qué van a llevar? Escucha y elige los dibujos apropiados. (1–5) (AT1/3) [8L3]

✕ *Listening for information/instructions, Level C*

Listening. Pupils listen to the recording and select the appropriate drawings.

Answers

1 b   **2** d   **3** e   **4** a   **5** c

Tapescript

1 *¿Qué vas a llevar para ir a la fiesta?*
   Voy a llevar pantalones y un top.
2 *¿Y tú? ¿Qué vas a llevar para ir a la fiesta?*
   Voy a llevar una falda.
3 *¿Qué vas a llevar para ir a la boda?*
   Voy a llevar un traje y una corbata.

4 *¿Y tú? ¿Qué vas a llevar a la boda?*
Voy a llevar un vestido muy elegante y zapatos de tacón alto.
5 *¿Vas a ir a la discoteca mañana?*
Sí, claro.
¿Qué vas a llevar?
Voy a llevar una sudadera …
… con capucha.
¡Por supuesto!

4 Empareja las dos partes correctas de cada frase. (AT3/3) [8W5]

✉ *Reading for information/instructions, Level C*

Reading. Pupils match the two parts of each sentence.

Answers

1 d	**2** c	**3** e	**4** b	**5** a	**6** f

5 Mira el cuadro y elige tres lugares. Escribe sobre la ropa que vas a llevar. (AT4/3) [8W4; 5; 8S7]

✉ *Exchange information/ideas, Level C/D*

Writing. Pupils write down what they are going to wear to go to various places.

ICT activity

'Newsletter' format. Report on what one or two celebrities are wearing to the Oscars.

Plenary [8W5]

Go round the class and ask pupils what they are going to wear to a party/other places.

¿Qué vas a llevar para ir a la fiesta? Voy a llevar …

Find someone who is willing to recite 'ir'.

Cuaderno A, page 27

1 Elige la descripción apropiada para cada dibujo. (AT3/2)

✉ *Reading for information/instructions, Level B*

Reading. Pupils choose the correct descripton for each picture, 1–4.

Answers

1 a	**2** a	**3** a	**4** b

2 Empareja las preguntas con las respuestas. (AT3/2) [8W5]

✉ *Reading for information/instructions, Level C*

Reading. Pupils match the questions, 1–5, with the answers, a–e.

Answers

1 b	**2** e	**3** a	**4** c	**5** d

3 Contesta a las preguntas. (AT4/2–3) [8W5; 8S2]

✉ *Exchange information/ideas, Level C/D*

Writing. Pupils answer questions 1–4 in Spanish.

Hojas de trabajo, Grammar, Resource and Assessment File, page 50

1

Using pronouns

Pupils complete sentences using the pronouns appropriate to the items to which they are referring.

Answers

a Me encanta la camiseta, ¿me *la* puedo probar?
b Odio los pantalones, no *los* quiero.
c ¿Dónde está la falda azul?, no *la* veo.
d Tengo una gorra negra, *la* llevo en invierno.
e Me gustan las zapatillas, ¿me *las* puedo probar?
f El uniforme es obligatorio, *lo* llevo en el instituto.

2

Infinitives

Pupils match up the 1st person singular form of each verb with its infinitive.

Answers

First Person	Infinitive
Voy	ir
Hago	hacer
Practico	practicar
Monto	montar
Salgo	salir
Llevo	llevar

Present and future

3

Pupils complete the grid giving the meaning of each verb in the 1st person singular and then putting them into the immediate future tense with the appropriate translation.

Answers

Present	Meaning	Immediate future	Meaning
Llevo	*I wear*	*Voy a llevar*	*I'm going to wear*
Voy a la discoteca	I go to the disco	Voy a ir la discoteca	I'm going to go to the disco
Monto a caballo	I go horseriding	Voy a montar a caballo	I'm going to go horseriding
Hago camping	I go camping	Voy a hacer camping	I'm going to go camping
Salgo con amigos	I go out with friends	Voy a salir con amigos	I'm going to go out with friends
Practico el ciclismo	I go cycling	Voy a practicar el ciclismo	I'm going to go cycling

4

Pupils write their own sentences about what they are going to do over the coming weekend using the immediate future tense.

5 ¿Llevas uniforme?

(Pupil's Book pages 50–51)

Main topics

- Talking about your school uniform
- Colours

Key Framework objectives

- Word endings 8W4 (Reinforcement)
- Connectives 8S2 (Launch)
- Daily life/young people 8C3 (Reinforcement)
- Text as model/source 8T6 (Launch)

Grammar

- Adjectives of colour
- Comparisons: *es más …, es menos …*

Key language

Para ir al instituto, llevo …
una chaqueta negra, una falda roja, unos pantalones grises, una camisa azul, un jersey verde, una corbata amarilla, unos zapatos negros

Es más/menos …
elegante   *barato*
cómodo   *caro*
práctico

Resources

Cassette B, side 1
CD 2, tracks 10 and 11
Cuaderno A, page 28

Starter 1 [8W4]

Aim: To practise colours and agreement of colours.

Write the following on the board or prepare an OHT.

(List these in two columns): *una corbata, unos pantalones, un jersey, unas zapatillas/negros, amarilla, rojas, verde*

Ask pupils to match the colours with the appropriate items of clothing. Write down what these are in English or draw a little picture and colour it in. Invite volunteers up to draw a line from the item of clothing to the correct colour.

1a Escribe el orden en que se menciona la ropa. (1–7) (AT1/2) [8L3]

✉ *Listening for information/instructions, Level A*

Listening. Pupils listen to the recording and write down the letter of the item of clothing.

Answers

1 a   2 d   3 g   4 f   5 b   6 e   7 c

Tapescript

1 *una chaqueta negra*
2 *una camisa azul*
3 *unos zapatos negros*
4 *una corbata amarilla y verde*
5 *una falda roja y marrón*
6 *un jersey verde*
7 *unos pantalones grises*

1b Juega al juego de la memoria. (AT2/2–3)

✉ *Speaking to convey information, Level C*

Speaking. Memory game. Working in pairs, pupils go over the items of clothing, adding one item each time.

2a Escucha y empareja las descripciones con los uniformes apropiados. (1–3) (AT1/3) [8L3; 8C3]

✉ *Listening for information/instructions, Level C*

Listening. Pupils listen to the recording and match the three people at the bottom of page 50 with the descriptions they hear.

Answers

1 a   2 c   3 b

Tapescript

1 *¿Llevas uniforme?*
   Sí, llevo una camisa blanca, una falda naranja y calcetines blancos.
2 *¿Llevas uniforme?*
   Sí, llevo una camisa blanca y una falda azul.
3 *¿Llevas uniforme al instituto?*
   No, no llevo uniforme.
   Pues, ¿qué llevas?
   Llevo vaqueros, una camiseta y zapatillas de deporte.

2b Mira los dibujos. Con tu compañero/a, pregunta y contesta. (AT2/2–3) [8W4; 8S2]

✉ *Speaking to convey information, Level C/D*

Speaking. Working in pairs or threes, pupils choose one of the students and describe their uniform as if they were wearing it. Example: *¿Llevas uniforme? Llevo …*

Suggestion

Pupils could choose one of the students but not tell their partner which one they have chosen. Describe the uniform. Their partner must try to guess who they are.

Starter 2 [8W4]

Aim: To recap agreement of colours.

Call out a list of clothes and hold up a different coloured pencil for each item of clothing. Ask pupils to write down the item of clothing and its colour: *una falda (roja), unos pantalones (negros)*, etc. Ask pupils to swap answers with a partner. Then go over the answers with them.

3a Lee los textos. ¿Verdad (✓) o mentira (✗)? (AT3/4)

✶ *Reading for information/instructions, Level D*

Reading. Pupils read the two letters from Daniel and Patricia. They then write down *verdad (✓) o mentira (✗)* for 1–7.

Answers

1 ✓	2 ✓	3 ✗	4 ✗	5 ✓	6 ✗	7 ✗

➕ Ask pupils to correct the answers that are false.

3b Lee los textos otra vez y escribe unas frases similares para describir tu uniforme. (AT4/3–4) [8S2; 8T6]

✶ *Exchange information/ideas, Level C–D*

Writing. Ask pupils to write down a few sentences to describe what they wear to school. Encourage pupils to extend sentences with *y*.

🖱 ICT activity

E-mail. Ask pupils to prepare an email to send to your link school about what they wear to school. Ask the link school to reply with a description of what they wear. They can then compare the two.

Plenary [8W4]

Write a colour on the board and the headings: masc. singular, fem. singular, masc. plural, fem. plural. Ask a volunteer to give you the variations or perhaps come up and fill them in. e.g.: *azul, verde, negro, amarillo* and a trick one like *naranja*. Can anyone name the other colours that don't change (*violeta, rosa*)?

En Casa

Personal dossier. Ask pupils to stick in a photo or draw a picture of themselves in school uniform and describe what they are wearing. Remind pupils to double check that the items of clothing and colours agree.

Cuaderno A, page 28

1a Lee las cartas y escribe M (Mariano) o S (Santiago) para cada dibujo. (AT3/3) [8W4; 8S2]

✶ *Reading for information/instructions, Level D*

Reading. Pupils read the two letters from Mariano and Santiago and write down M or S for pictures 1–8.

Answers

1 S	2 M	3 M	4 M	5 M	6 S	7 M

1b Contesta a las preguntas. (AT3/3) [8W4; 8S2]

✶ *Reading for information/instructions, Level D*

Reading. Pupils answer questions 1–7 in English.

Answers

1 blue	2 shoes	3 blue and yellow
4 he doesn't like it, it's not practical		
5 jeans, t-shirt, sweatshirt (with hood), trainers		
6 trainers		
7 it's convenient and practical		

1c Escribe unas frases para describir tu uniforme. (AT4/2–3) [8T5]

✶ *Exchange information/ideas, Level B/D*

Writing. Pupils use the template to help them describe their uniform.

If they don't wear a uniform, ask them to make one up!

6 En la calle principal

(Pupil's Book pages 52–53)

Main topics

- Talking about types of shops
- Saying where you can buy things

Key Framework objectives

- Modal verbs 8S3 (Launch)
- Verb tenses (near future) 8W5 (Reinforcement)

Other aims

- Pronunciation practice

Grammar

- Present tense of *poder: puedo, puedes*

Key language

¿Dónde puedo comprar …?

Puedo/puedes comprar … en …
la zapatería   *la farmacia*
la librería   *la frutería*
la panadería   *la tienda de regalos*
la carnicería   *la tienda de discos*
las tiendas españolas
  de moda

Resources

Cassette B, side 1
CD 2 tracks 12 and 13
Cuaderno A, page 29
Starter 1, Resource and Assessment File, page 47
OHTs 19, 20

Starter 1

Aim: Vocabulary extension: working out the meaning of words using cognates, near cognates and knowledge of other vocabulary.

Use *Resource and Assessment File*, page 47. Ask pupils to deduce the meaning of the following places (cognates): *la librería, la farmacia, la frutería, la tienda de discos*

Work out the meaning of the following places by relating them to words they already know: *la panadería, la carnicería, la zapatería*

This is a good opportunity to work on correct stress.

1a Escribe el orden en que se mencionan las tiendas. (1–9) (AT1/1)

✕ *Listening for information/instructions, Level A*

Listening. Pupils listen to the recording and match sentences 1–9 with the appropriate picture (a–i).

Answers

1 b	2 h	3 e	4 g	5 f	6 i	7 c	8 d	9 a

Tapescript

1 *La librería*
2 *Las tiendas españolas de moda*
3 *La farmacia*
4 *La tienda de regalos*
5 *La frutería*
6 *La tienda de discos*
7 *La panadería*
8 *La carnicería*
9 *La zapatería*

1b Escucha. ¿En que tiendas puedes comprar estos artículos? (1–6) (AT1/2) [8L3]

✕ *Listening for information/instructions, Level B*

Listening. Pupils listen to the recording and write down the names of the shops where they can buy the items on page 52.

Answers

1 panadería	2 zapatería	3 librería	4 farmacia
5 frutería	6 carnicería		

Tapescript

1 *¿Dónde puedo comprar pan?*
  Puedes comprar pan en la panadería.
2 *¿Dónde puedo comprar zapatos?*
  Puedes comprar zapatos en una zapatería.
3 *¿Dónde puedo comprar libros?*
  Puedes comprar libros en una librería.
4 *¿Dónde puedo comprar aspirinas?*
  Puedes comprar aspirinas en una farmacia.
5 *¿Dónde puedo comprar manzanas?*
  Puedes comprar manzanas en la frutería.
6 *¿Dónde puedo comprar chuletas?*
  Puedes comprar chuletas en la carnicería.

1c Con tu compañero/a, pregunta y contesta (AT2/2) [8S3]

✕ *Speaking and interacting with others, Level C*

Speaking. Working in pairs, pupils ask and answer where they can buy different items.

Starter 2

Aim: Pronunciation practice.

Remind pupils that in Spanish you tend to use short vowels and in English (depending on where you come from) you often use long vowels. Go over the difference between long and short vowels. Now ask pupils to work with a partner and practise saying the names of the shops and the things you can buy there.

2a Lee la postal de Charo. Copia y completa el cuadro con la información apropiada (AT3/5)

✕ *Reading for information/instructions, Level D*

Reading. Pupils copy the grid on page 53, read Charo's postcard and fill in the grid accordingly.

Answers

Persona	Regalo	Tienda
madre	abanico	tienda de recuerdos
abuela	castañuelas	tienda de recuerdos
abuelo	cerámica	tienda de recuerdos
padre	CD	tienda de discos
hermana	camiseta	tienda española de modas

2b ¿Qué vas a comprar, para quién y dónde? Escribe una lista. (AT4/5) [8W5; 8S6]

✕ *Exchange information/ideas, Level C/D*

Writing. Ask pupils to write sentences about what presents they are going to buy for their families and where they can buy them.

Plenary

Discuss ways of learning vocabulary.

If pupils are short of ideas take them through the following:

1 LOOK	Look carefully at the word for at least 10 seconds.
2 SAY	Say the word to yourself/out loud to practise pronunciation.
3 COVER	Cover up the word when you feel you have learned it.
4 WRITE	Write the word from memory.
5 CHECK	Check your word against the original. Did you get it right? Repeat the steps until you've learned the word.

Cuaderno A, page 29

1 Empareja los artículos con las tiendas apropiadas. (AT3/1)

✕ *Reading for information/instructions, Level A*

Reading. Pupils match the items, a–f, with the correct shops, 1–6.

Answers

1 c 2 e 3 a 4 d 5 f 6 b

2 Contesta a las preguntas. (AT3/2, 4/2)

✕ *Exchange information/ideas, Level C*

Reading and writing. Pupils answer questions 1–5.

Answers

> 1 Puedo comprar un diccionario en una librería.
> 2 Puedo comprar pollo en una carnicería.
> 3 Puedo comprar naranjas en una frutería.
> 4 Puedo comprar aspirinas en una farmacia.
> 5 Puedo comprar pan en una panadería.

3 Lee el texto y contesta a las preguntas. (AT3/4)

✕ *Reading for information/instructions, Level D*

Reading. Pupils read the text about the presents Nicolás is going to buy members of his family for Christmas. Answer questions 1–7 in English.

Answers

> 1 CD 2 Mum 3 gift shop 4 clothes shop 5 t-shirt
> 6 chocolates 7 sweet shop

módulo 3

Resumen y Prepárate

(Pupil's Book pages 54–55)

Resumen

This is a checklist of language covered in Module 3. There is a comprehensive *Resumen* list for Module 3 in the Student's Book (page 54) and a *Resumen* test sheet in *Cuaderno* A (page 33).

Key Framework objectives

● Verb tenses (near future) 8W5 (Reinforcement)

Prepárate

A revision test to give practice for the test itself at the end of the module.

Resources

Cassette B, side 1
CD 2, track 14
Cuaderno A, pages 30, 31, 32 and 33
Resumen, Resource and Assessment File, page 52
Skills, Resource and Assessment File, page 51

1 Escucha las conversaciones. Copia y rellena el cuadro. (1–5) (AT1/3) [8L3]

✕ *Listening for information/instructions, Level C*

Listening. Pupils listen to the conversations and fill out the grid.

Answers

	Artículo	Número/Talla
1	botas	42
2	camisa	36
3	vaqueros	40
4	vestido	34
5	zapatos	38

Tapescript

1 – ¿Me puedo probar esas botas?
– ¿Qué número usa usted?
– El 42.
– Aquí tiene.
2 – Me encanta esa camisa. ¿Me la puedo probar?
– ¿Qué talla usa?
– La 36.
– La 36 … Tome usted.
3 – Aquellos vaqueros no son caros. ¿Me los puedo probar?
– ¿Qué talla usa?
– La 40.
– La 40. Aquí tiene.
4 – Aquel vestido verde es precioso.
– ¿Se lo quiere probar?
– ¡Ay, sí!
– ¿Qué talla usa?
– La 34.
– La 34. Tome usted.
5 – ¿Me puedo probar estos zapatos?
– Sí, cómo no. ¿Qué número usa?
– El 38.
– El 38. Aquí tiene.

2a Mira los dibujos. Con tu compañero/a, pregunta y contesta. (AT2/2–3) [8W5; 8S2]

✕ *Speaking and interacting with others, Level C/D*

Speaking. Role-play. Pupils ask each other what they are going to wear to the disco.

2b Mira los dibujos. Con tu compañero/a, pregunta y contesta. (AT2/2)

✕ *Speaking and interacting with others, Level C/D*

Speaking. Role-play. Pupils ask each other where they can buy the six items.

3 Empareja las frases con los dibujos. (AT3/2)

✕ *Reading for information/instructions, Level C*

Reading. Pupils match the sentences with the drawings.

Answers

1 e **2** d **3** h **4** a **5** g **6** c **7** b **8** f

4 Escribe una frase para cada dibujo. (AT4/2) [8W4]

✕ *Reading for information/instructions, Level A*

Writing. Pupils write a sentence to describe 1–7.

Cuaderno A, page 30

Repaso 1

1a Mira el dibujo y marca los artículos de la lista. (AT3/2)

✕ *Reading for information/instructions, Level A*

Reading. Pupils look at the drawing and tick the items on the list.

Answers

1 falda **3** camiseta estampada **5** sandalias **6** gafas de sol **9** chaqueta

1b Escribe dos listas. (AT4/2)

✕ *Exchange information/ideas, Level B/C*

Writing. Pupils write two lists of the clothes they will take for a holiday in Cuba and a holiday in Canada.

Cuaderno A, page 31

Repaso 2

1a Lee la conversación. ¿Verdad (✓) o mentira (✗)? (AT3/3)

✕ *Reading for information/instructions, Level D*

Reading. Pupils read the conversation and mark true (✓) or false (✗) for 1–5.

Answers

1 ✗   2 ✓   3 ✓   4 ✗   5 ✓

1b Mira los dibujos y escribe una conversación similar. (AT4/3–4)

✕ *Writing imaginatively, Level C/E*

Writing. Pupils use pictures 1–4 to write a similar conversation.

Answers (*example*)

> Me gusta esta camiseta blanca. ¿Me la puedo probar?
> Claro. ¿Qué talla tiene?
> La cuarenta y dos.
> Tome usted.
> ¿Cuanto cuesta?
> Quince euros.
> Me la llevo.

Cuaderno A, page 32

Gramática

1a Write *este, esta, estos* or *estas*. [8W4]

✕ *Knowing about language*

Answers

1 esta   2 estas   3 estos   4 este

1b Write *ese, esa, esos* or *esas*. [8W4]

✕ *Knowing about language*

Answers

1 esos   2 ese   3 esas   4 esa

1c Write *aquel, aquella, aquellos* or *aquellas*. [8W4]

✕ *Knowing about language*

Answers

1 aquel   2 aquellos   3 aquella   4 aquellas

2 Answer the questions using the listed objects.

✕ *Knowing about language*

Writing. Pupils answer questions 1–5 in Spanish using the items in the box.

Answers

> 1 Voy a comprar pan en el supermercado.
> 2 Voy a comprar una raqueta de tenis en la tienda de deporte.
> 3 Voy a comprar cerámica en la tienda de regalos.
> 4 Voy a llevar vaqueros y una sudadera para ir a la fiesta.
> 5 Voy a llevar pantalones cortos para jugar al tenis.

Skills, Resource and Assessment File, page 51 (Ordering and sorting words)

1

1	*amarillo*	*yellow*
2	azul	blue
3	blanco	white
4	gris	grey
5	marrón	brown
6	naranja	orange
7	negro	black
8	rojo	red
9	rosa	pink
10	verde	green
11	violeta	purple

2

Carnicería	Farmacia	Frutería	Ropa	Deportes
carne	aspirinas	manzanas	camisa	baloncesto
chuletas	champú	naranjas	camiseta	fútbol
jamón	colonia	plátanos	gorra	natación
pollo	desodorante	uvas	pantalones	voleibol

Answers

3

Pupils fill in the grid giving three examples of words that fall into each grouping: animals, family, colours, hobbies.

4a

Answers

> **1** zapatos **2** lechuga **3** cafetería **4** azul **5** cuatro
> **6** pájaro

4b

Answers

> **1** *Wear on your feet; plural*
> **2** It's a vegetable – the others are fruits/It's singular, the others are plural
> **3** You buy food to eat *there*. In the other two you buy food to eat somewhere else.
> **4** It's a colour – the others are sizes
> **5** It's a cardinal number – the others are ordinal.
> **6** It's a bird – the others are animals

4c

Answers

> **1** You wear them.
> **2** You eat them.
> **3** They are adjectives.
> **4** They are numbers.
> **5** They are pets.

7 ¡Extra! ¿Cuál es tu estilo?

(Pupil's Book pages 56–57)

This is an optional extension unit which reviews some of the key language of the module: it is a 'style' test from a Teen magazine.

Key Framework objectives

- Dictionary detail 8W7 (Launch)
- Authentic text as source 9T3 (Reinforcement)
- Youth attitudes to sport/popular culture 9C3 (Launch)

Resources

Cassette B, side 1
CD 2, track 15

Starter 1 [8W7; 8T4]

Aim: Glossary practice.

Write up the following words (from the text in **1a**).

botas, bailar, la música étnica, película, mochila, teléfono móvil, dinero, feo

Ask pupils to:
1 Write down what they think the word means or might mean.
2 Check the meaning in the glossary.
3 Write down whether the word is a verb, a noun or an adjective.

1a Escucha y lee el test. Elige las letras apropiadas. (AT1/2) [9C3]

✂ *Listening for information/instructions, Level C*

Listening/Reading. Pupils listen to and follow the test at the top of page 56. They then choose the most appropriate answers from a–d for numbers 1–6.

Answers

1 c	2 d	3 c	4 a	5 c	6 b

Tapescript

1 – ¿Cuáles son tus colores preferidos?
– Por el momento prefiero el negro, el rojo y el violeta.
2 – ¿Cuáles son tus zapatos favoritos?
– Mis zapatillas Nike.
3 – ¿Qué te gusta más hacer los fines de semana?
– Me encanta salir a bailar.
4 – ¿Qué tipo de música prefieres?
– Me gustan Moby y trip hop.
5 – ¿Cuáles son tus accesorios más importantes?
– Mi accesorio más importante es mi teléfono móvil.
6 – ¿Cuál es tu opinión sobre el uniforme escolar?
– Creo que el uniforme escolar es feo.

1b Lee el análisis otra vez. ¿Cuál es el estilo personal de la persona en **1a**? (AT3/4) [9C3]

✂ *Reading for information/instructions, Level D/E*

Reading. Pupils look at the analysis on page 57 and write down what sort of style the person in **1a** has.

---

2 Con tu compañero/a, contesta a las preguntas del test y busca tu estilo en el análisis. (AT2/2–3)

✂ *Experiences, feelings, opinions, Level C/D*

Speaking. Working in pairs, pupils answer the questions on the style test for themselves and then look at the analysis to see which one fits them.

Starter 2 [8W7; 8T4]

Aim: Verbs.

Ask pupils to find three verbs from the test, look them up in the dictionary and write down what the infinitives are and what they mean.

3a Escribe cuatro frases del test que corresponden a tu estilo personal. (AT4/2) [9T3]

✂ *Exchange information/ideas, Level B*

Writing. Pupils write down four sentences from the test that suit their own style.

3b Escribe dos frases del análisis que corresponden a tu compañero/a. (AT4/3) [9T3]

✂ *Exchange information/ideas, Level C/D*

Writing. Pupils write down two sentences from the test that suit their partner's style.

Plenary [9T4]

Find out how pupils tackled the test. Did they dive straight in and start to answer the questions? Or, did they take time to look up words in the dictionary? Did they deduce meaning from context? Think about cognates? Use grammar points covered so far? What method do pupils think works best?

● Self-access reading and writing at two levels

A Reinforcement

1a Empareja las frases con los dibujos. (AT3/2) [8S4]

✉ *Reading for information/instructions, Level D*

Reading. Pupils match 1–5 with the drawings (a–e).

Answers

1 e	2 c	3 a	4 b	5 d

1b Empareja las preguntas de **1a** con las respuestas. (AT3/2) [8S4]

✉ *Reading for information/instructions, Level D*

Reading. Pupils match questions 1–5 in **1a** with the answers (a–e).

Answers

1 b	2 d	3 c	4 e	5 a

2 Mira los dibujos. Copia y completa las descripciones. Elige las palabras de la lista. (AT3/3) [8W4, 5]

Reading/writing. Pupils look at the drawings and choose words to fill in the gaps and complete the descriptions (1–4).

Answers

1 a negro **b** blanca
2 a cortos **b** camiseta
3 a falda **b** zapatos
4 a gorra **b** gafas
5 a vaqueros **b** blancas

B Extension

1a Empareja los dibujos con las frases. (AT3/2) [8W1]

✉ *Reading for information/instructions, Level C*

Reading. Pupils match the drawings (1–8) with sentences a–h.

Answers

a 4	b 3	c 8	d 5	e 2	f 6	g 7	h 1

1b Mira los dibujos en **1a**. ¿Cuál prefieres y por qué? ¿Cuál no te gusta y por qué? (AT4/4) [8S2]

✉ *Exchange information/ideas, Level D/E*

Writing. Pupils look at the drawings in **1a** and write down which ones they prefer and why/which ones they don't like and why.

módulo 4 El turismo

(Pupil's Book pages 60–75)

Unit	Key Framework objectives	PoS	Key language and Grammar
1 ¿Qué hay de interés? (pp. 60–61) Talking about what there is to see Naming places of interest Talking about the weather	8W8 Non-literal meanings [L] 8T1 Meanings in context [L] 8T5 Continuous text [L] 9C5 Region of the country [L] 8S4 Question types [R]	2e adapt language 2f adapt language for different contexts 3d use reference materials 4c compare cultures 5e range of resources 5f using the TL creatively 5h using the TL for real purposes	There is, there are: *hay* *¿Qué hay de interés en …?* *Hay (un parque temático).* *Hace (buen tiempo). Llueve. Nieva.*
2 Tus vacaciones (pp. 62–63) Saying where you go on holiday Saying how you get there Saying who you go with	8W5 Verbs (present) [R] 8S4 Question types [R] 8L3 Relaying gist and detail [R]	2a listen for gist and detail 2c ask and answer questions 2d initiate/develop conversations 5e range of resources	The verb *ir*: *voy a, voy en, voy con* *¿Dónde vas de vacaciones normalmente?* *Voy a (un camping).* *¿Cómo vas?* *Voy en (autocar).* *¿Con quién vas?* *Voy con (mis padres).*
3 ¿Qué haces? (pp. 64–65) Talking about where you go on holiday Talking about what you do on holiday Talking about how you get there	8W5 Verbs (present) [R] 8S2 Connectives [R] 8S4 Question types [R] 8T1 Meaning in context – *hacer* [R] 8T5 Continuous text [R]	2a listen for gist and detail 3d use reference materials 4b communicating with native speakers 5d respond to different types of language 5e range of resources	Irregular verbs: *Ir: voy, vas, va* *Hacer: hago haces, hace* *Jugar: juego, juegas, juega* Regular verbs: *Tomar: tomo, tomas, toma* *(descansar, montar, nadar)* *¿Qué haces durante las vacaciones?* *Descanso, nado en el mar, …* *¿Dónde vas de vacaciones normalmente?/¿Cómo vas?/ ¿Con quién vas?/ ¿Qué haces?*
4 Fuimos al parque temático (pp. 66–67) Saying where you and your friends went Saying when you went and at what time of day	8T2 Expression in text [L] 8W5 Verbs (preterite) [L] 8S7 Present, *past, future* [L] 8L4 Extending sentences [R]	2j redraft writing 5e range of resources	The preterite of *ir*: *fui, fuiste, fue, fuimos, fuisteis, fueron* Fui and *fuimos* used actively Prepositions: *al/ a la* *Fui (a la piscina). Fuimos (al centro comercial).* *El sábado por la mañana … El domingo por la tarde …*
5 Mis vacaciones del año pasado (pp. 68–69) Saying what you did on holiday	8W5 Verbs (preterite) [R]		The preterite: -*ar* verbs *Fui de vacaciones a (España).* *Fui en (avión).* *Me alojé/Nos alojamos en (un hotel).* *Visité (un castillo).* *Compré (una camiseta).* *Me lo pasé (fenomenal).*
Resumen y Prepárate (pp. 70–71) Pupil's checklist and practice test	8W5 Verbs (present, preterite) [R] 8S2 Connectives [R] 8T5 Writing continuous text [R]		
6 ¡Extra! ¡Cuba! (pp. 56–57) Optional unit: Cuba	8S8 High-frequency words [L] 9C4 Features of the country [L] 8W5 Verbs (preterite) [R] 8W7 Dictionary detail [R] 8T5 Writing continuous text [R]	2h scanning texts 3d use reference materials 4c compare cultures 4d consider experiences in other countries 5d respond to different types of language	*¿Qué hiciste?* *Jugué al golf, al tenis, al voleibol.* *Practiqué la vela. Nadé en el mar.* *Bailé salsa. Monté en bicicleta.* *Cené en un restaurante. Descansé en la playa.* *Tomé el sol. Fui de compras.*
Te toca a ti (pp. 114–115) Self-access reading and writing at two levels	8W5 Verbs (present, preterite) [R]		

Main topics

- Asking what there is to see in a place
- Naming places of interest
- Talking about the weather

Key Framework objectives

- Non-literal meanings 8W8 (Launch)
- Meanings in context 8T1 (Launch)
- Continuous text 8T5 (Launch)
- Region of the country 9C5 (Launch)
- Question types 8S4 (Reinforcement)

Grammar

- There is, there are: *hay*

Key language

¿Qué hay de interés en …?
Hay …

un parque temático	*una feria de caballos*
espectáculos de flamenco	*pistas de tenis*
una plaza de toros	*centros comerciales*
playas	*muchos restaurantes*
campos de golf	*un zoo*
un puerto	*muchos monumentos*
hace buen tiempo	*hace mal tiempo*
hace sol	*hace calor*
hace frío	*hace viento*
llueve	*nieva*

Resources

Cassette B, side 2
CD 2, track 16
Cuaderno A, page 34
Starter 2, Resource and Assessment File, page 67
Flashcards 26–30 and 52, 55, 59, 69 and 73 (*¡Listos! 1*)

Starter 1

Aim: Using the high frequency word *hay* in different contexts revise language pupils have already met in *iListos! 1.*

Write on the board or ask your pupils the following question(s):

¿Qué hay en tu dormitorio? Or *¿Qué hay en tu pueblo?*

Ask pupils to spend a few minutes writing a list of things in their room/town and then tell their partner. They can then share answers with the class.

Suggestion

Revise weather using flashcards 76–86 from *Listos 1*. Introduce some places of interest using flashcards 26–30 from *iListos! 2* (*espectáculos de flamenco, un parque temático, los campos de golf, una feria de caballos* and *pistas de tenis*). When you have introduced these places and practised the language with your class you could play the guessing game: *¿Qué hay de interés?* Pupils must try to guess which cards you are holding: *¿Hay un/una …? Sí, toma* (hand card to pupils). *No* (move to next volunteer).

Revise *¿Cómo es tu ciudad/pueblo?* (from *Listos 1* – Flashcards 67–75). Give pupils a couple of minutes to think about/remember adjectives to describe their town. Example: *antiguo/grande/interesante. Hay un castillo.* Brainstorm: Ask pupils to tell you what their thoughts are and write them down under the headings *Mi ciudad es …, Hay un/una …* See how much they can remember!

1a Escucha y lee. Escribe los lugares de interés en el orden correcto. (AT1/3) [8W8; 8L3; 9C5]

✂ *Listening for information/instructions, Level D*

Listening/Reading. Pupils listen to the recording and look at the maps of Jerez de la Frontera and Málaga. Ask them to write down the numbers of the places of interest for each town in the order in which they are mentioned. If you haven't introduced the new places with the Flashcards, check for meaning before playing the recording. *El centro comercial, la plaza de toros, las playas, los monumentos* and *un puerto* are revised from Book 1.

Answers

Jerez de la Frontera: 3, 1, 2	Málaga: 1, 3, 2

Tapescript

¿Qué hay de interés en Jerez de la Frontera?
Bastante cerca hay un parque temático.
¿Hay playas?
No, pero hay espectáculos de flamenco y hay una plaza de toros.

¿Qué hay de interés en Málaga?
Hay muchas playas y un puerto.
¿Hay campos de golf?
Sí, hay muchos campos de golf.

1b Con tu compañero/a, pregunta y contesta. (AT2/2–3) [8W8; 8S4]

✂ *Speaking and interacting with others, Level C/D*

Speaking. Working in pairs, pupils take it in turns to ask and answer questions about the two towns.

Aim: Revising weather.

Use the word snake on page 67 of the *Resource and Assessment File*. Ask pupils to identify as many weather phrases as they can (*Hace buen tiempo, hace sol, hace frío, llueve, hace mal tiempo, hace calor, hace viento, nieva*).

2a Lee los diálogos y contesta a las preguntas. Utiliza un diccionario. (AT3/4) [8W8; 8T4; 9C5]

✄ *Reading for information/instructions, Level D*

Reading. Pupils read the two descriptions of Jerez de la Frontera and Málaga at the top of page 61 and answer questions 1–7 in Spanish. Remind them to use a dictionary if they get stuck.

2b Con tu compañero/a, pregunta y contesta. (AT2/2–4) [8W8; 8S4, 6]

✄ *Speaking and interacting with others, Level C/D*

Speaking. Working in pairs, pupils talk about places of interest in their part of the world.

2c En el ordenador diseña un folleto para tu ciudad/pueblo. (AT4/3–4) [8W8; 8S6; 8T5, 6]

✄ *Writing imaginatively, Level C/E*

Writing. Pupils use a computer to design a leaflet describing places of interest in their town.

➕ **Drama** Bring in posters of some famous cities and stick them on the board. Ask pupils to sit in a double circle facing each other. They take it in turns to choose a city and ask questions. Give no more than five minutes for these conversations then clap your hands and pupils in the inner circle must move one place to their right. Pupils on the outer circle must also move one place to their right (hopefully a complete change of partners!). Do this a few times. Conversations should become a bit more detailed as pupils find out more and more about what there is to see in each city. (These could be Paris, New York, Madrid, London).

✎ **ICT activity**

Set up an e-mail link with your partner school and compare towns. What is there to see and do?

Video diary. Ask pupils to work in small groups of four and make a video diary of their town to send to your partner school. Liaise with your partner school and see if it would be possible for them to do one as well. Tip: check with your IT coordinator for ways to ensure that this project runs smoothly.

What do pupils notice about the way questions are asked in Spanish (definite change in intonation towards the end of the question, voice becomes higher)? Is this different to the way we ask questions in English?

Ask pupils to think of some questions they have just met in this unit. Get them to ask you these questions putting the correct emphasis on the words.

En casa

Personal dossier. Ask pupils to up-date their personal dossier. Write a small description of their town, draw pictures to illustrate what it is like or add some photos.

Cuaderno A, page 34

1a ¿Qué hay de interés en Cádiz? Lee el texto y elige los dibujos apropiados. (AT3/4)

✄ *Reading for information/instructions, Level D*

Reading. Pupils read the text about places of interest in Cádiz and tick the relevant pictures, 1–9.

Answers

2, 3, 4, 5, 8, 9

1b ¿Qué tiempo hace en Cádiz? Marca los símbolos apropiados. (AT3/4)

✄ *Reading for information/instructions, Level D*

Reading. Pupils tick the appropriate weather symbols, 1–4, to show what the weather is like in Cádiz.

Answers

3 and 4

2 Mira los dibujos y completa la descripción de Sevilla. (Mira las palabras subrayadas en **1a**.) (AT4/2) [8S6]

✄ *Reading for information/instructions, Level D*

Reading. Pupils fill in the gaps and complete the description of Seville. Hint: look at the underlined words in activity **1a**.

Answers

Monumentos, plaza de toros, restaurantes, espectáculos de flamenco, playas, parque temático, hace sol, hace calor, hace frío

2 Tus vacaciones

(Pupil's Book pages 62–63)

Main topics

- Saying where you go on holiday
- How you go
- Who you go with

Key Framework objectives

- Verb tenses (present) 8W5 (Reinforcement)
- Question types 8S4 (Reinforcement)
- Relaying gist amd detail 8L3 (Reinforcement)

Grammar

- The verb *ir: voy a, voy en, voy con*

Key language

¿Dónde vas de vacaciones normalmente?
Voy …

a un camping	*a un pueblo*
a la costa	*al campo*

¿Cómo vas?
Voy en …

coche	*tren*
avión	*autocar*

¿Con quién vas?
Voy con mi(s) …
padres/familia/amigo(s)

Resources

Cassette B, side 2
CD 2, tracks 17 and 18
Cuaderno A, page 35

Starter 1 [8W5]

Aim: To revise *ir*.

Use a fluffy toy/ball: Throw this to a pupil at random and give him/her a subject pronoun: e.g. *yo*. The pupil replies with *voy* and throws the toy back. Throw the toy to another pupil and repeat the process. Go through the paradigm for *ir* several times, increasing the pace.

Suggestion

Quickly revise transport using flashcards 23–29 from *¡Listos! 1*. Or bring in some props and ask pupils what they are. *¿Qué es? Un coche, un tren*, etc.

1a Escucha. Copia y rellena la ficha. (1–4) (AT1/3) [8L3]

✉ *Listening for information/instructions, Level C*

Listening. Pupils listen to the recording and fill in the grid with the appropriate information: where to and how.

Answers

	¿Dónde?	¿Cómo?
Carlota	la costa	avión
Miguel	pueblo	tren
Penélope	campo	coche
José Luis	camping	autocar

Tapescript

1 – Carlota, ¿Dónde vas de vacaciones normalmente?
  – Normalmente voy a la costa.
  – ¿Cómo vas?

– Voy en avión.
  – ¿Con quién vas?
  – Voy con mi familia.
2 – ¿Dónde vas de vacaciones normalmente, Miguel?
  – Normalmente voy a un pueblo.
  – ¿Cómo vas?
  – Voy en tren.
  – ¿Con quién vas?
  – Voy con mis padres.
3 – Penélope, ¿Dónde vas de vacaciones normalmente?
  – Normalmente voy al campo.
  – ¿Cómo vas?
  – Voy en coche.
  – ¿Con quién vas?
  – Voy con mis padres.
4 – ¿Dónde vas de vacaciones normalmente, José Luis?
  – Normalmente voy a un camping.
  – ¿Cómo vas?
  – Voy en autocar.
  – ¿Con quién vas?
  – Voy con mis amigos.

1b Escucha otra vez. ¿Con quién van? (AT1/3) [8L3]

✉ *Listening for information/instructions, Level C*

Listening. Pupils listen to the recording again and write down who they are going with.

Answers

Carlota: familia   **Miguel:** padres   **Penélope:** padres
José Luis: amigos

Tapescript

As for activity **1a**

Starter 2

Aim: Holiday places.

Write the following anagrams on the board or prepare an OHT: **1** le amopc (*el campo*) **2** al socta (*la costa*) **3** un bloeup (*un pueblo*) **4** sal ñasatmno (*las montañas*) **5** nu cgnpima (*un camping*)

2 Con tu compañero/a, mira los dibujos, pregunta y contesta. (AT2/3–4) [8S4]

✉ *Speaking and interacting with others, Level C/D*

Speaking. Working in pairs, pupils look at the three pictures and take it in turns to ask and answer questions about them.

3a Lee los textos y copia y rellena la ficha. (AT3/3)

✉ *Reading for information/instructions, Level C*

Reading. Pupils look at the three texts and fill out the grid with information about where Juan, Clara and Carlos go on holiday.

Answers

	Where?	Who with?	How?
Juan	un camping	amigos	tren
Clara	la costa	familia	autocar
Carlos	un pueblo	padres	coche

3b Lee los textos otra vez y escribe frases similares sobre tus vacaciones. (AT4/3–4) [8S6]

✉ *Exchange information/ideas, Level C/E*

Writing. Ask pupils to use the text in **3a** to write a similar one of their own. Where do they go on holiday? How do they travel? And who do they go with?

🔊 **ICT activity**

Ask pupils to do activity **3b** on a word processor or desktop publisher. They could include a photo or drawing.

Plenary

Ask pupils how you would say: I'm going by … (*Voy en …*), I'm going to the … (*Voy al …/a la …*) I'm going with … (*Voy con …*) to focus their attention on the different prepositions.

1 Lee las frases. ¿Quién habla? (AT3/2)

✉ *Reading for information/instructions, Level C*

Reading. Pupils use the grid to help them write down who is speaking in sentences 1–8.

Answers

1 Juan	**2** Marina/Pablo	**3** Tamara
4 Marina/Juan/Pablo	**5** Marina	**6** Tamara
7 Juan	**8** Pablo	

2 Imagina que vas de vacaciones. Mira los dibujos y escribe frases sobre tus vacaciones. (AT4/2–4) [8W5]

✉ *Writing imaginatively, Level C/E*

Writing. Pupils use the pictures to help them write a few sentences about an imaginary holiday.

Answers (*example*)

Normalmente voy de vacaciones a la playa.
Voy con mi familia. Vamos a un camping/Vamos a la costa. Vamos en coche.

3 ¿Qué haces?

(Pupil's Book pages 64–65)

Main topics

- Talking about where you go and what you do on holiday
- Saying how you get there

Key Framework objectives

- Verb tenses (present) 8W5 (Reinforcement)
- Connectives 8S2 (Reinforcement)
- Question types 8S4 (Reinforcement)
- Meanings in context 8T1 (Reinforcement)
- Continuous text 8T5 (Reinforcement)

Grammar

- Irregular verbs:
  Ir: voy, vas, va
  Hacer: hago, haces, hace
  Jugar: juego, juegas, juega
- Regular verbs:
  Tomar: tomo, tomas, toma
  (descansar, montar, nadar)

Key language

Descanso.	*Voy a discotecas.*
Nado en el mar.	*Monto en bicicleta.*
Tomo el sol.	*Saco fotos.*
Voy de paseo.	*Hago surfing*

¿Dónde vas de vacaciones?
¿Cómo vas?
¿Con quién vas?
¿Qué haces?

Resources

Cassette B, side 2
CD 2, track 19
Cuaderno A, page 36
Hojas de trabajo, Resource and Assessment File, pages 69 and 70 (*descansar, nadar, ir de paseo, montar en bici, ir de compras, tomar el sol, sacar fotos, hacer surfing*)
Flashcards 31–38
OHTs 21, 22

Starter 1 [8W5]

Aim: Revision and conjugation of regular –*ar* verbs.

Write the following on the board: *descanso, tomo, voy, nado, monto*

Ask pupils to spot the odd one out (*voy*). What group do the other verbs belong to? Ask pupils to choose two and conjugate: *yo, tú, él/ella*

What do they mean?

Suggestion
Introduce holiday activities using the flashcards and OHTs.

1a Escucha. ¿Qué hacen estas personas durante las vacaciones? Elige los números correctos. (1–4) (AT1/3) [8L3; 8TI]

✗ *Listening for information/instructions, Level C*

Listening. Pupils listen to the recording and write down which activities each person practises when he/she is on holiday.

Answers

Carlota: 2,3,5   Miguel: 1,7,6   Penélope: 1,2,4
José Luis: 3,5,8

Tapescript

1 – Carlota, ¿Qué haces durante las vacaciones?
 – Nado en el mar, tomo el sol y voy a discotecas.
2 – ¿Qué haces durante las vacaciones, Miguel?
 – Descanso, saco fotos y monto en bici.

3 – Penélope, ¿Qué haces durante las vacaciones?
 – Descanso, nado en el mar y voy de paseo.
4 – José Luis, ¿Qué haces durante las vacaciones?
 – Tomo el sol, voy a discotecas y hago surfing.

1b En grupos, mira los dibujos en **1a** y pregunta y contesta. (AT2/3) [8W5; 8S4]

✗ *Speaking and interacting with others, Level C/D*

Speaking. Working in groups of no more than four and using the labelled pictures in **1a**, pupils find out what activities other class members like to do when on holiday.

ICT activity

MS Excel. Carry out a class survey or group survey to find out the most popular holiday activities. Enter the data and use the chart wizard to produce a pie chart.

Starter 2 [8W5]

Aim: To recap holiday activities.

Write the following parts of sentences on the board in two columns and ask pupils to match them up correctly.

1 *voy, nado, monto, hago, saco*

2 *fotos, en el mar, surfing, de paseo, en bicicleta*

2a Lee el correo electrónico y empareja las dos partes de las frases. Utiliza un diccionario. (AT3/4) [8W5]

✉ *Reading for information/instructions, Level D*

Reading. Pupils read the e-mail and match the two parts of the sentences. Ask pupils to use a dictionary to help them.

Answers

1 f	**2** b	**3** g	**4** a	**5** h	**6** c	**7** e	**8** d

2b Escribe una respuesta al correo electrónico de Isidro. (AT4/3) [8S2, 6; 8T5]

✉ *Writing to establish/maintain contact, Level C/E*

Writing. Pupils answer Isidro's e-mail using the writing frame.

3a Haz un sondeo. Pregunta a tus compañeros/as de clase. (AT2/3–4) [8S4]

✉ *Speaking and interacting with others, Level D/E*

Speaking. Pupils carry out a class survey: Where do they go (*¿Dónde vas de vacaciones?*)? How do they travel (*¿Cómo vas?*)? Who do they go with (*¿Con quién vas?*)? What do they do (*¿Qué haces?*)? Encourage pupils to use *normalmente* and *generalmente*.

💬 **ICT activity**

Word processing. Ask pupils to work with a partner and produce a form to record answers on. Use rows and columns, enter the field names and print out.

3b En el ordenador, haz gráficos con los resultados del sondeo. (AT4/3)

✉ *Exchange information/ideas, Level C/D*

Writing. Pupils use a computer programme, for example MS Excel, to record results from the survey and produce graphs.

💬 **ICT activity**

E-mail. Send a survey to your link school and compare results.

Plenary [8W5]

Ask the class how you would say: I go surfing, I go for a walk, I sunbathe, I rest.

Now ask volunteers how you would say the same things in the *tú* form.

What is the pattern for regular –*ar* verbs?: *yo, tú, él/ella*

Cuaderno A, page 36

1 Lee los textos y escribe 'Sam' o 'Jaime' para cada dibujo. (AT3/4) [8W5; 8T3]

✉ *Reading for information/instructions, Level D*

Reading. Pupils read the two letters from Sam and Jaime. Then write the name of the appropriate person under pictures 1–6.

Answers

1 Sam	**2** Sam	**3** Jaime	**4** Sam	**5** Sam	**6** Sam

2 ¿Verdad (✓) o mentira (✗)? (AT3/4) [8W5]

✉ *Reading for information/instructions, Level D*

Reading. True or False.

Answers

1 ✓	**2** ✓	**3** ✗	**4** ✗	**5** ✓	**6** ✓

3a ¿Qué contesta Jaime a estas preguntas? Escribe sus respuestas. (AT4/2–3) [8W5]

✉ *Exchange information/ideas, Level B*

Writing. Pupils write down Jaime's answers to questions 1–3.

Answers

1 Voy a un pueblo pequeño en la costa.
2 Voy con mi familia.
3 Juego al tenis, voy a los bares y restaurantes, bailo, voy a la playa y tomo el sol.

3b Escribe tus propias respuestas a las preguntas en **3a**. (AT4/2–4) [8W5]

✉ *Writing to establish/maintain contact, Level C/E*

Writing. Pupils write their own answers to the questions in activity **3a**.

Hojas de trabajo, Resource and Assessment File, pages 69 and 70

Cards for pairwork featuring weather and holiday activities: pupils match the pictures to the correct words.

4 Fuimos al parque temático

(Pupil's Book pages 66–67)

Main topics

- Saying where you and your friends went
- Saying what day you went and time of day

Key Framework objectives

- Verb tenses (preterite) 8W5 (Launch)
- Present, *past*, future 8S7 (Launch)
- Expression in text 8T2 (Launch)
- Extending sentences 8L4 (Reinforcement)

Grammar

- The preterite of *ir: fui, fuiste, fue, fuimos, fuisteis, fueron*
- *Fui* and *fuimos* used actively
- Prepositions: *al/a la*

Key language

Fui/fuimos …
al centro comercial   *a un parque temático*
al parque   *a un partido de fútbol*
al polideportivo   *a la piscina*
al cine   *a la playa*
El sábado por la mañana, el domingo por la tarde

Resources

Cassette B, side 2
CD 2, tracks 22 and 23
Cuaderno A, page 37
Flashcards *¡Listos!* 1 52, 53, 54, 56, 59, 62

Starter 1

Aim: To practise the preposition 'to the': *al/a la*

Have ready on the board the following list of places:

centro comercial, parque, piscina, cine, playa, polideportivo, parque temático, partido de fútbol

Ask pupils to list these in two columns under *al* and *a la*. Ask them to use the glossary if they are not sure of the gender of a noun or what it means (The last two items are new).

Suggestion

Quickly revise places using Flashcards 52, 53, 54, 56, 59 and 62 from *¡Listos!* 1. Example: *¿Qué es? Una piscina*, etc.

1 Escucha y escribe los dibujos en el orden correcto. (1–8) (AT1/2)

✂ *Listening for information/instructions, Level B*

Listening. Pupils listen to the recording and put drawings in the correct order (a–h).

Answers

1 f	**2** g	**3** a	**4** b	**5** d	**6** c	**7** h	**8** e

Tapescript

1 *Fui al parque.*
2 *Fuimos al cine.*
3 *Fui a la piscina.*
4 *Fuimos al centro comercial.*
5 *Fui al polideportivo.*
6 *Fuimos a la playa.*
7 *Fuimos a un partido de fútbol.*
8 *Fuimos a un parque temático.*

2 Escucha y escribe *fui o fuimos*. (1–8) (AT1/2) [8L1]

✂ *Listening for information/instructions, Level B*

Listening. Pupils listen to the recording and write down *fui* or *fuimos*. (1–8)

Answers

1 fui	**2** fui	**3** fuimos	**4** fuimos	**5** fui	**6** fui	**7** fuimos
8 fui						

Tapescript

1 *Fui a España.*
2 *Fui al río.*
3 *Fuimos a Francia.*
4 *Fuimos a la montaña.*
5 *Fui a Londres.*
6 *Fui al campo.*
7 *Fuimos a Estados Unidos.*
8 *Fui a Australia.*

Starter 2 [8W5]

Aim: To recap *fui* and *fuimos*.

Ask pupils to stand in a circle (or simply stand up). Throw a soft ball to a pupil giving the English 'I went' or 'we went'. Pupils respond with the Spanish and throw the ball back. If someone drops the ball or makes a mistake they must sit down.

3a Con tu compañero/a, mira los dibujos y habla del fin de semana. (AT2/4–5) [8W5; 8S1; 8L4]

✂ *Experiences, feelings, opinions, Level D/E*

Speaking. Working in pairs, pupils look at the four pictures at the top of page 67 and talk about what they did at the weekend.

3b Escribe cinco frases sobre los dibujos en **3a**. (AT4/4) [8W5; 8S1,7; 8L4]

✉ *Exchange information/ideas, Level D/E*

Writing. Pupils write five sentences about the drawings in **3a**.

👄 **ICT activity**

Word processing. Pupils could word process this activity. Corrections can be made later.

4 Copia y completa con las palabras apropiadas. (AT3/5) [8W5; 8T2]

✉ *Reading for information/instructions, Level E*

Reading. Pupils copy and fill in the gaps with appropriate words chosen from the bubble.

Answers

> **1** fui **2** parque temático **3** cerca **4** coche
> **5** amigos **6** tren **7** fuimos

Plenary [8W5]

Ask pupils if they can think of a good strategy to help them remember the preterite of *ir*. Take feedback.

Get them to give you some of the time phrases they have used in the unit: *El sábado por la mañana/por la tarde, El sábado pasado*, etc.

Cuaderno A, page 37

1 Mira los dibujos y escribe frases con las palabras del cuadro. (AT4/2) [8W5]

✉ *Reading for information/instructions, Level C*

Reading. Pupils choose appropriate sentences from the writing grid to go with pictures 1–6.

Answers

> **1** Fuimos al parque temático.
> **2** Fui a la piscina.
> **3** Fuimos al cine.
> **4** Fui al polideportivo.
> **5** Fuimos a la playa.
> **6** Fuimos al centro comercial.

2 Lee el texto y completa el diario de Vanessa. (AT3/3) [8W5]

✉ *Reading for information/instructions, Level D*

Reading. Pupils read the text and complete Vanessa's diary.

Answers

		¿Adónde?	¿Con quién?
el sábado	a.m.	a la piscina	–
	p.m.	al centro comercial	una amiga
el domingo	a.m.	al parque	el perro
	p.m.	al cine	sus padres

5 Mis vacaciones del año pasado

(Pupil's Book pages 68–69)

Main topics

● Saying what you did on holiday

Key Framework objectives

● Verb tenses (preterite) 8W5 (Reinforcement)

Grammar

● The preterite: -ar verbs

Key language

Fui de vacaciones a (España).
Fui en (avión).

Visité (un castillo).
Compré (una camiseta).
Lo pasé (fenomenal).

Resources

Cassette B, side 2
CD 2, tracks 22 and 23
Cuaderno A, page 38
Grammar, Resource and Assessment File, page 71
OHTs 23, 24
Dice

Starter 1 [8W5]

Aim: To recap the preterite. Using *fui* in three different sentences.

Ask pupils to write down: **1** Where they went on Saturday. **2** Who they went with. **3** How they travelled there.

1a Escucha y escribe los números apropiados. (1–5) (AT1/2) [8W5; 8L3]

✉ *Listening for information/instructions, Level C*

Listening. Pupils listen to the recording and look at the grid at the top of page 68. They then write down the appropriate numbers for 1–5.

Answers

1 3	2 1	3 5	4 1	5 2

Tapescript

1 *El año pasado fui de vacaciones a Estados Unidos.*
2 *Fui en avión.*
3 *Visité un parque temático.*
4 *Compré una camiseta.*
5 *Lo pasé muy bien.*

1b Con tu compañero/a, tira el dado y habla de tus vacaciones. (AT2/4–5) [8W5]

✉ *Speaking and interacting with others, Level D*

Speaking. Working in pairs, pupils take it in turns to throw the dice and talk about their holidays. The number of dots on the dice relate to the numbers on the grid (e.g. if you get six dots you talk about number 6 on the grid).

---

2 Escucha y escribe los dibujos en el orden correcto. (1–6) (AT1/2) [8W5]

✉ *Listening for information/instructions, Level C*

Listening. Pupils listen to the recording and write down the letters of the drawings in the correct order.

Answers

1 b	2 f	3 e	4 c	5 a	6 d

Tapescript

1 *Fui de vacaciones a Francia con mis padres.*
2 *Fuimos en coche.*
3 *Nos alojamos en un camping.*
4 *Me bañé en el mar.*
5 *Compré una gorra.*
6 *Visité un castillo.*

Starter 2 [8W5]

Aim: To recap the first person in the preterite tense.

Write on the board the following: *El sábado fui a …, fui en …, visité …, compré …, lo pasé …*

Ask pupils to fill in the gaps. Encourage them to do this activity without looking at their books.

---

3 Copia y completa las frases con las palabras apropiadas. (AT3/4) [8W5]

✉ *Knowing about language*

Reading. Pupils copy the text and fill in the gaps.

Answers

1 fui	2 me alojé	3 visité	4 compré	5 me bañé

---

4 Escribe seis frases sobre tus vacaciones. (AT4/4–5) [8W5]

✉ *Exchange information/ideas, Level D/E*

Writing. Ask pupils to write down where they went for their holidays last year. Use the grid on page 68 as a template.

Cuaderno A, page 38

1 Empareja las frases. (AT 3/5) [8W5]

❌ *Reading for information/instructions, Level D*

Reading. Pupils match the sentences.

Answers

1 c 2 h 3 a 4 e 5 d 6 g 7 f 8 b

2 Elige los tres dibujos apropiados para Claudia. (AT3/5) [8W5]

❌ *Reading for information/instructions, Level D*

Reading. Pupils use activity **1** to help them choose appropriate drawings on the grid to show what Claudia did on her holiday.

Answers

3 Mira los dibujos y escribe frases para describir las vacaciones. (AT4/5) [8W5]

❌ *Exchange information/ideas, Level D/E*

Writing (preterite). Pupils look at the six drawings and choose words from the box to describe the holiday.

Answers

1 Fui de vacaciones a Austria.
2 Fui en tren.
3 Me alojé en un hotel.
4 Me bañe en la piscina.
5 Visité un castillo.
6 Compré un gorro de lana.

Grammar, Resource and Assessment File, page 71 (The preterite tense)

1

Pupils fill in the blanks in a grid to give various –ar verbs in their infinitive and preterite forms (1st

Infinitive	Meaning	Preterite	Meaning
Alojarse	*To stay*	*Me alojé*	*I stayed*
Bañarse	*To swim*	*Me bañé*	*I swam*
Comprar	*To buy*	*Compré*	*I bought*
Nadar en el mar	*To swim in the sea*	*Nadé en el mar*	*I swam in the sea*
Pasarlo bomba	*To have a great time*	*Lo pasé bomba*	*I had a great time*
Visitar	*To visit*	*Visité*	*I visited*

person singular) together with their meanings.

Answers

2

Pupils rearrange the words to make complete sentences.

Answers

a Visité un castillo con mis amigos.
b El sábado por la mañana fui a la piscina.
c Me alojé en un hotel maravilloso el año pasado.
d Me baño en la playa el jueves.
e Me lo pasé bomba en la fiesta.
f Antes de volver a casa compré unos regalos.

3

Pupils read a number of sentences and tick those which are in the past tense.

Answers

b, c and e

módulo 4

Resumen y Prepárate

(Pupil's Book pages 70–71)

Resumen

This is a checklist of language covered in Module 4. There is a comprehensive *Resumen* list for Module 4 in the Pupil's Book (page 70) and a *Resumen* test sheet in Cuaderno A, (page 43)

Prepárate

A revision test to give practice for the test itself at the end of the module.

Key Framework objectives

- Verb tenses (preterite) 8W5 (Reinforcement)
- Connectives 8S2 (Reinforcement)
- Writing continuous text 8T5 (Reinforcement)

Resources

Cassette B, side 2
CD 2, track 24
Cuaderno A, pages 39, 40, 41, 42 and 43
Resumen, Resource and Assessment File, page 75
Skills, Resource and Assessment File, page 73

---

1 Escucha y escribe los lugares en el orden correcto. (1–6) (AT1/2) [8L3]

✖ *Listening for information/instructions, Level C*

Listening. Pupils listen to the recording and write down the places in the correct order for 1–6.

Answers

1 b	2 e	3 a	4 c	5 f	6 d

Tapescript

1 – *¿Qué hay de interés en Málaga?*
– *Hay un puerto.*
2 – *¿Qué hay de interés en Sevilla?*
– *Hay espectáculos de flamenco.*
3 – *¿Qué hay de interés en Jerez de la Frontera?*
– *Hay una plaza de toros.*
4 – *¿Dónde hay campos de golf?*
– *Hay muchos campos de golf cerca de Málaga.*
5 – *¿Dónde hay una fiesta de caballos?*
– *¿Una fiesta de caballos? En Jerez.*
6 – *¿Qué hay de interés cerca de tu pueblo?*
– *Hay un zoo.*

2a Con tu compañero/a, empareja las preguntas con las respuestas. [8S4]

✖ *Speaking and interacting with others, Level C*

Speaking. Working in pairs, pupils match the questions and answers.

Answers

1 e	2 d	3 b	4 a	5 c

2b Pregunta y contesta para ti. (AT2/3–4) [8S2, 4]

✖ *Speaking and interacting with others, Level C/D*

Speaking. Working in pairs, pupils answer the questions about themselves.

---

3 Lee y contesta a las preguntas. (AT3/5) [8W5]

✖ *Reading for information/instructions, Level E*

Reading. Pupils read the letter and answer questions (1–8) in English.

4 Completa las frases para describir tus vacaciones. (AT4/4) [8W5; 8S2; 8T5]

✖ *Writing to establish/maintain contact, Level D/E*

Writing. Pupils copy the sentences and fill in the gaps with their own information to write about their holidays.

Cuaderno A, page 39/40

Repaso

1 Lee el diálogo y elige las frases correctas de Susa. (AT3/5) [8W5]

✖ *Reading for information/instructions, Level E*

Reading. Pupils read the conversation about Susa's holiday in Seville. Ask pupils to choose appropriate speech bubbles, 1–10, to describe her holiday.

Answers

1, 2, 6, 7, 8, 9

2 ¿Qué hay de interés en Sevilla? Escribe una lista. (AT4/2–3, AT3/5)

✖ *Exchange information/ideas, Level B/C*

Writing and reading. Pupils write a list of places of interest in Seville.

Answers

En Sevilla hay un parque temático, una plaza de toros, una catedral, museos, restaurantes, parques (bonitos) y piscinas.

3 ¿Qué hace Susa normalmente cuando va de vacaciones? ¿Y en Sevilla? Marca los dibujos apropiados. (AT3/5) [8W5]

✂ *Reading for information/instructions, Level E*

Reading. Pupils tick the boxes on the grid to show what Susa ususally does on holiday and the boxes to show what she did in Seville.

Answers

Normalmente: 1, 2, 6
En Sevilla: 3, 5, 8, 9

4 Escribe las palabras en los espacios para saber el nombre del parque temático en Sevilla. (AT3/4)

✂ *Reading for information/instructions, Level D*

Reading. Pupils choose words from the box to fill in gaps for sentences 1–10. When they have finished they should look at the letters in the highlighted boxes to find out what the name of the theme park in Seville is.

Answers

1 bonitos **2** Sevilla **3** plaza **4** abril **5** llama **6** temático **7** agradable **8** fiesta **9** flamenco **10** ciudad
El parque temático se llama **isla mágica**.

Cuaderno A, page 41

Gramática 1

1 Complete the sentences with the correct verb: *hay* or *hace*. [8S8]

✂ *Knowing about language*

Answers

1 hay **2** hay **3** hace **4** hace **5** hay **6** hace **7** hay

2a Choose the first person singular form of each of the following verbs. [8W5]

✂ *Knowing about language*

Answers

1 hago **2** voy **3** monto **4** nado **5** saco **6** tomo

2b Use the appropriate verbs from **2a** to complete these sentences. [8W5]

✂ *Knowing about language*

Answers

1 nado **2** voy **3** monto **4** hago **5** saco **6** voy

2c Write sentences about what you do and don't do on holiday. [8W5; 8S5]

✂ *Knowing about language*

Writing. Pupils write sentences about their holidays in the present tense.

3 Write a sentence for each picture. [8W5]

✂ *Knowing about language*

Writing. Pupils write a sentence in the preterite tense for each picture, 1–6.

Answers

1 Fui al estadio.
2 Fui al parque.
3 Fui a la piscina.
4 Fui al mercado.
5 Fui al cine.
6 Fui en tren.

Cuaderno A, page 42

Gramática 2

1 Match the questions and answers. [8W5]

✂ *Knowing about language*

Writing. Pupils match sentences in the preterite.

Answers

1 f **2** d **3** b **4** e **5** c **6** a

2 Complete the paragraph with the correct verbs. [8W5; 8S6]

✂ *Knowing about language*

Answers

1 fui **2** Fui **3** Me alojé **4** Me bañé **5** Visité **6** Compré **7** Lo pasé

3 Write sentences about a holiday you went on. [8W5; 8T5]

✂ *Knowing about language*

Skills, Resource and Assessment File, page 73 (Word associations and analogies)

1

Answers

> **a** *Como en un restaurante.*
> **b** Juego al fútbol/al tenis.
> **c** Nado en la piscina/en el mar.
> **d** Viajo en avión/en coche.
> **e** Visito mis amigos/mis abuelos.
> **f** Compro una bicicleta/un sombrero.

2

Answers

> **a** *derecha*
> **b** Inglaterra
> **c** tarde
> **d** fui
> **e** nieva
> **f** pequeño - moderno

3

Answers

> **a** *viento*
> **b** fútbol
> **c** avión
> **d** hermana
> **e** fatal

6 ¡Extra! ¡Cuba!

(Pupil's Book pages 72–73)

Main topics

This is an optional extension unit which reviews some of the key language of the module and extends it through texts about a visit to Cuba.

Key Framework objectives

- High-frequency words 8S8 (Launch)
- Verb tenses (preterite) 8W5 (Reinforcement)
- Dictionary detail 8W7 (Reinforcement)
- Writing continuous text 8T5 (Reinforcement)
- Features of the country 9C4 (Launch)

Key language

¿Qué hiciste?
Jugué al golf, al tenis, al voleibol.

Practiqué vela.
Bailé salsa.
Cené en un restaurante.
Tomé el sol.
Nadé en el mar.
Monté en bicicleta.
Descansé en la playa.
Fui de compras.

Resources

Cassette B, side 2
CD 2, tracks 25 and 26
Starter 1, Resource and Assessment File, page 68

Starter 1 [8S8]

Aim: To revise some useful high frequency words.

Make an OHT using *Resource and Assessment File,* page 68. Put the OHT on your projector upside down and 'back to front' with the wrong side showing. Ask your pupils to work in pairs to decipher what the words are and also write down what they mean in English. Remind pupils to use a dictionary if they are unsure. These words all appear in the text on Cuba.

es, muy, la, hay, también, los, una, como, y, en las, tiene, el

Answers

> **1** 8 hours   **2** old American cars
> **3** a long street next to the sea
> **4** bars, restaurants, squares, hotels, airport   **5** wonderful
> **6** hot and sunny   **7** tobacco plantations   **8** beisbol

Starter 2

Aim: To build confidence prior to tackling the diary text in activity **2a**.

Ask pupils to look at the diary on page 73 and find the Spanish for: in the morning, in the afternoon, we went to the beach, my parents played golf, we went to the disco, we went to the countryside.

1 Lee el texto sobre Cuba y contesta a las preguntas. Busca las palabras que no conoces en el diccionario. (AT3/5) [8W4, 7; 8T7; 9C4]

✖ *Reading for information/instructions, Level E*

Reading. Approach the text by asking pupils to scan it for words or phrases that are familiar. Give them two minutes to find as many items as they can. Pool the group's findings.

Now write down a list of words for pupils to look up in the glossary.

isla, viaje, tocan, plaza, nocturna, bonita, bordea

Ask them to **1** write down the meaning **2** say whether it is a noun, a verb or an adjective **3** if a noun, whether it is masculine or feminine and **4** if a verb, give the infinitive.

Ask pupils to read the leaflet again and answer questions (1–8) in English. Get them to use a dictionary for words they are unsure about.

2a Lee el diario de Miguel en la página 73. Copia y rellena el cuadro. (AT3/5) [8W5]

✖ *Reading for information/instructions, Level E*

Reading. Pupils look at Miguel's diary and fill in the grid with the appropriate information.

Tapescript

	Viernes		Sábado		Domingo	
	mañana	tarde	mañana	tarde	mañana	tarde
Miguel	nadamos	bici	vela	bailar	caballo	
Claudia	nadamos	tenis	vela	bailar	voleibol	ir de compras
Padre	nadamos	tenis	vela	golf	caballo	
Madre	nadamos	tenis	vela	golf	playa	ir de compras

2b Lee el diario otra vez. Escucha y escribe el día apropiado. (1–6) (AT1/4) [8W5; 8L3]

✖ *Listening for information/instructions, Level D*

Reading/Listening. Pupils look at the diary again and listen to the recording. They then write down the correct day for 1–6.

Answers

1 domingo	**2** viernes	**3** sábado	**4** viernes	**5** viernes	
6 domingo					

Tapescript

1 *Fui al campo.*
2 *Monté en bici.*
3 *Bailé salsa.*
4 *Jugué al tenis.*
5 *Fui a la playa y nadé en el mar.*
6 *Jugué al voleibol y fui de compras.*

2c Eres Miguel o Claudia. Con tu compañero/a, pregunta y contesta. (AT2/5) [8W5; 8S4]

✖ *Speaking and interacting with others, Level D/E*

Speaking. Working in pairs, pupils play the roles of Miguel and Claudia. They take it in turns to ask and answer questions. Their partner must guess who they are.

3 Fuiste de vacaciones a Cuba. Escribe unas frases describiendo lo que hiciste. (AT4/5) [8W5; 8T5, 6]

✖ *Writing imaginatively, Level D/E*

Writing. Pupils pretend they have been to Cuba (or perhaps they really have been on holiday there!). Ask them to write down a description of what they did.

Encourage more able pupils to use connectives and time phrases, using Miguel's diary as a source of language.

Plenary [8W7; 8T4]

Brainstorm. Ask pupils what strategies they use to look up a word in the glossary/dictionary if it is: **1** an adjective **2** a verb **3** a noun

Escucha y lee la canción y busca las palabras que no conoces en el diccionario. [8C4]

✖ *Listening for enjoyment*

Listening. Pupils listen to the song and look up any unfamiliar words in the dictionary.

Tapescript

¡Cuba!
*Fui en avión,
de vacación.
fui a la playa
en la costa de Cuba.*

*Muy bien lo pasé,
con recuerdos regresé.
Hizo muy buen tiempo
y nunca hizo viento.*

*Fui a un bar
muy cerca del mar.
tomé un café caliente
y me puse a ver la gente.
Vi a un inglés
hablar con un francés
y un jamaicano
charlar con un cubano.*

*Mojitos bebí,
helados comí,
mangos y papayas,
piñas y guayabas
Un día cené
en la Fonda San José
arroz y pollo frito
que estaba muy rico.*

*En una discoteca
Conocí una chica
Bailamos salsa
Hasta la madrugada.
La chica me encantó,
muy bien bailó.
Manuela se llamaba
en la playa trabajaba.*

*En el mar me bañé,
deportes practiqué.
Con mi Manuela
aprendí a hacer la vela.
El water ski,
el buceo aprendí.
Con mi instructora
me puse en buena forma.*

*El fin llegó,
Manuela se despidió.
Prometí no olvidarla
y escribirle una carta.
En casa estoy,
Ahorrando voy
para ir a la playa
en la costa de Cuba.*

Te toca a ti

(Pupil's Book pages 114–115)

● Self-access reading and writing at two levels.

Key Framework objectives

● Verb tenses 8W5 (Reinforcement)

A Reinforcement

1a ¿Qué hay de interés en Alicante? Elige los dibujos apropiados. (AT3/4)

✉ *Reading for information/instructions, Level D*

Reading. Pupils read the text about Alicante and tick the appropriate pictures of things to do there.

Answers

a e f g h

1b ¿Qué tiempo hace en Alicante? (AT3/4)

✉ *Reading for information/instructions, Level D*

Reading. Pupils choose the picture which best describes what the weather is like in Alicante.

Answers

a Hace sol.

2 Mira la información en el cuadro y lee las frases. Elige tres frases para cada persona. (AT3/3) [8W5]

✉ *Reading for information/instructions, Level D*

Reading. Pupils look at the grid and the sentences. Ask them to write down three sentences for each person to describe their holiday.

Answers

Pedro: Voy de vacaciones al campo. Voy a un camping. Voy con mi familia. Voy en coche. **Isabel:** Normalmente voy de vacaciones a la costa. Voy con mis amigos. Voy en tren.

3 Escribe seis frases sobre tus vacaciones. (AT4/4)

Writing. Pupils write six sentences about things they do on holiday.

B Extension

1a Empareja los textos con los dibujos. (AT3/5) [8W5]

✉ *Reading for information/instructions, Level E*

Reading. Pupils match the three letters with the three pictures.

Answers

1 b 2 c 3 a

1b ¿Quién habla? Escribe G (Guillermo), M (Max) o S (Susa) para cada frase. (AT3/5) [8W5]

✉ *Reading for information/instructions, Level E*

Reading. Pupils write down the initial of the person to go with 1–8.

Answers

1 M 2 G 3 S 4 M 5 M 6 S 7 G 8 G

2 Escribe sobre un viaje. Elige las palabras de cada grupo para completar las frases. (AT4/5) [8W5; 8S6]

✉ *Writing imaginatively, Level D/E*

Writing. Ask the pupils to write some sentences about a holiday they remember. Encourage them to use expressions from the pie chart.

módulo 5 ¡Diviértete!

(Pupil's Book pages 76–91)

Unit	Key Framework objectives	PoS	Key language and Grammar
1 ¿Quieres ir al cine? (pp. 76–77) Arranging to go out with a friend Arranging a time and a place Time of day	8L6 Expressions in speech [L] 8S4 Question types [R] 8C5 Colloquialisms [R]	2a 2c 2d	*¡Diga! ¿Quieres ir (al club de jóvenes)?* *¿Cuándo? A las siete.* *¿Dónde quedamos? En (la plaza).* *Bueno, vale, buena idea.* *Esta mañana/ esta tarde/esta noche/mañana por la mañana/mañana por la tarde*
2 ¿Qué tipo de películas te gustan? (pp. 78–79) Saying what type of films you like/dislike Saying why you like them	8W2 Connectives [L] 9W1 Word discrimination [L] 8L5 Unscripted speech [L] 8W1 Adding abstract words [R] 9C3 Youth attitudes to sport/popular culture [R]	1a sounds and writing 2b pronunciation/ intonation 2c ask and answer questions 2i report main points 3a memorising 4a working with authentic materials 5c express opinions 5e range of resources	Adjectives: *aburrido(a)(s)/emocionante(s)/…* *¿Qué tipo de películas prefieres?* *(No) Me gustan/Prefiero las películas (románticas).* *Porque (no) son (emocionantes).*
3 Dos entradas por favor (pp. 80–81) Buying tickets at the cinema Asking about film times Discussing film categories	9T5 Creative writing [L]	2a listen for gist and detail 2e adapt language 3b use context to interpret meaning 4a working with authentic materials 5f using TL creatively 5h using TL for real purposes	*Dos entradas por favor.* *¿Para qué película? Para Las Dos Torres.* *¿Para qué sesión? Para la sesión de las siete y media.* *Aquí tiene.* *¿Cuánto es? Son (once euros).* *Apta para todos los públicos/para mayores de 7 años/ para mayores de 13 años/ para mayores de 18 años*
4 ¡Es genial! (pp. 82–83) Describing an event in the present tense	9S4 Building answers from questions [L] 8W5 Verb tenses (present) [R] 8S7 *Present*, past, future [R] 8T2 Explanations in text [R] 8L6 Expressions in speech [R] 9C5 Region of the country [R]	2c ask and answer questions 2d initiate/develop conversations 2e adapt language 4b communicating with native speakers 4c compare cultures 4d consider experiences in other countries 5e range of resources	*Estoy en (el Museo del Prado).* *Estoy con (mis amigos).* *Hace (mal tiempo).* *Es (divertido).*
5 ¿Qué hiciste el sábado? (pp. 84–85) Describing an event in the past	8W5 Verbs (preterite) [R] 8S7 Present, *past*, future [R]	2c ask and answer questions 2d initiate/ develop conversations 5e range of resources	Regular *–er* and *–ir* verbs: *Comer: comí, comiste, comimos* *Salir: salí, saliste, salimos* Irregular verbs: *Hacer: hice, hiciste, hicimos* *Ver: vi, viste, vimos* *Salí de casa (a las cinco y media).* *Fui (en tren).* *Vi un partido entre (Real Madrid y Valencia).* *Comí (patatas fritas).* *Bebí (un café con leche).* *Vi a (Raúl).*

módulo 5 ¡Diviértete!

Unit	Key Framework objectives	PoS	Key language and Grammar
Resumen y Prepárate (pp. 86–87) Pupil's checklist and practice test	8S7 Present, past, future [R]		
6 ¡Extra! ¿Qué tal era? (pp. 88–89) Optional unit: using the imperfect tense to describe the weather.	8W5 Verbs (preterite) [R] 8S4 Question types [R] 8S7 Present, past, future [R]	2h scanning texts	*Hacía sol/ hacía calor/ hacía viento/ hacía mal tiempo* *Había mucha gente* *¡Era fenomenal!* *¡Era un desastre!*
Te toca a ti (pp. 116–117) Self-access reading and writing at two levels	8S1 Word, phrase, clause sequencing [R] 8S7 Present, past, future [R] 8T6 Text as model [R]		

módulo 5

1 ¿Quieres ir al cine?

(Pupil's Book pages 76–77)

Main topics

- Arranging to go out with a friend
- Arranging a time and a place
- Time of day

Key Framework objectives

- Expression in speech 8L6 (Launch)
- Question types 8S4 (Reinforcement)
- Colloquialisms 8C5 (Reinforcement)

Key language

¿Quieres ir ...?
al club de jóvenes   al cine
a la bolera   al parque de atracciones
a la pista de hielo

¿Cuándo?
A las siete.
¿Dónde quedamos?
En la plaza/En tu casa/En la estación.
Bueno/Vale/Buena idea.
esta mañana   mañana por la mañana
esta tarde   mañana por la tarde
esta noche

Resources

Cassette C, side 1
CD 3, tracks 2 and 3
Cuaderno A, page 44
Hojas de trabajo, Resource and Assessment File, pages 90 and 91
Flashcards 39–42

Starter 1

Aim: To recap places of interest in a town.

Ask pupils to work with a partner and write down as many places of interest as they can think of. Set a time limit (no looking up!). Take feedback and write these on the board.

Suggestion

Introduce the vocabulary using Flashcards 39–42.

1 Empareja los lugares con los dibujos. (AT3/1)

✖ *Reading for information/instructions, Level A*

Reading. Pupils match the places (1–5) with the drawings (a–e). (They should be able to deduce *el cine*.)

Answers

1 c 2 e 3 d 4 b 5 a

2 Lee la conversación y contesta a las preguntas. (AT3/4)

✖ *Reading for information/instructions, Level D*

Reading. Pupils look at the telephone conversation and answer questions 1–4.

Answers

1 the cinema 2 Saturday 3 in the square 4 at seven

3a Escucha. ¿Adónde van los amigos y cuándo van a salir? (1–4) (AT1/4) [8C5; 8L3]

✖ *Listening for information/instructions, Level D*

Listening. Establish the meaning of *esta mañana/tarde/noche*. Pupils listen to the recording and write down in English where the friends are going and when.

Answers

1 this afternoon, youth club	2 Sunday, ice rink
3 tonight, amusement park	4 this afternoon, bowling

Tapescript

1 – ¿Diga?
– Hola, Javier. Soy Felipe.
– Hola Felipe.
– ¿Quieres ir al club de jóvenes?
– ¿Cuándo?
– Esta tarde.
– Buena idea.

2 – ¿Diga?
– Hola, Santiago. Soy Elena. ¿Quieres ir a la pista de hielo el domingo?
– ¿Cuándo?
– ¿El domingo?
– Bueno.

3 – ¿Diga?
– Hola, Mónica. Soy Raúl. ¿Quieres ir al parque de atracciones esta noche?
– ¿Cuándo?
– Esta noche.
– Sí, buena idea.

4 – ¿Diga?
– Hola, Alejandra. Soy Marta.
– Hola Marta. ¿Qué tal?
– Bien, bien. Mira. ¿Quieres ir al club de jóvenes?
– ¿Cuándo?
– ¿Esta tarde?
– No, prefiero ir a la bolera.
– Bueno, pues vamos a la bolera.

1 ¿Quieres ir al cine?

módulo 5

Starter 2

Aim: To revise telling the time.

Using mini whiteboards or paper, ask pupils to draw a clock face. Say a time in Spanish. Pupils draw the hands in and hold up the clock to show you. Do six of these; you could give times of morning activities. e.g. *Me levanto a las 6.30. Me ducho a las 6.45, tomo el desayuno a las 7.00.* If pupils are using paper, get them to draw six clock faces. Ask pupils to swap papers with a partner when finished to correct them.

3b Con tu compañero/a, pregunta y contesta. (AT2/3) [8S4; 8C5]

✄ *Speaking and interacting with others, Level D/E*

Speaking. Working in pairs, pupils arrange to go out.

3c ¿A qué hora y dónde se encuentran los amigos? (1–4) (AT1/4) [8L3]

✄ *Listening for information/instructions, Level D*

Listening. Pupils listen to the recording and write down the time and place for 1–4.

Answers

1 5.30/bar	2 9.00/their house	3 7.30/cafeteria
4 6.00/station		

Tapescript

1 – ¿A qué hora quedamos?
  – A las cinco y media.
  – Bueno. ¿Dónde quedamos?
  – En el bar.
  – Vale.
  – Hasta luego.
  – Adiós.
2 – ¿A qué hora quedamos?
  – ¿A las nueve?
  – Vale, a las nueve. ¿Dónde quedamos?
  – ¿En tu casa?
  – Bueno, aquí en mi casa.
  – Hasta luego.
  – Adiós.
3 – ¿A qué hora quedamos?
  – ¿A las ocho?
  – No, mejor a las siete y media.
  – Vale. ¿Dónde quedamos?
  – ¿En la cafetería?
  – Bueno, en la cafetería.
  – Hasta luego.
  – Hasta luego.
4 – ¿A qué hora quedamos?
  – ¿A las seis?
  – Vale. ¿Dónde quedamos?
  – ¿En la estación?
  – Muy bien.

– Adiós.
– Hasta luego.

3d Con tu compañero/a, pregunta y contesta. (AT2/3) [8S4; 8L6]

✄ *Speaking and interacting with others, Level D/E*

Speaking. Working in pairs, pupils take it in turns to ask their partner at what time they are going to meet and where. Encourage them to add expression with phrases such as *¿Diga?, Vale, Hasta luego,* etc.

➕ **Drama.** Making arrangements to go out. Pupils form an outer circle and an inner circle. They sit down facing each other and say where they are going, give a time and a meeting place. They write down the key information. After a few minutes clap your hands. All pupils move one seat to their right and arrange to go out with someone else. At the end of this activity ask pupils what their preferred choice is.

4 Lee los mensajes y escribe las palabras que faltan. (AT4/3)

✄ *Exchange information/ideas, Level C*

Writing. Pupils read the telephone messages and fill in the missing words.

Answers

bolera	sábado/noche	ocho y media	estación	casa.

5 Lee la conversación en **2** otra vez y escribe otra similar. (AT4/4)

✄ *Exchange information/ideas, Level C/E*

Writing. Pupils read the conversation in exercise **2** and write a similar one. They can do this in pairs.

🖭 ICT activity

Recording/CD recording. Ask pupils to record a telephone conversation with their partner arranging to go out. They should state a time and a meeting place.

Plenary

Ask pupils if they can remember useful phrases for a (telephone) conversation e.g. *¿Diga?, muy bien, vale, adiós.*

Ask them to think of strategies to help them make a telephone call in another language (prepare what you are going to say very carefully), what should you do whilst having the conversation (have pen and paper to hand, jot down notes so you don't forget anything)? If the person is speaking too fast what are two useful phrases (*más despacio por favor, puede repetir por favor*)?

módulo 5 1 ¿Quieres ir al cine?

Cuaderno A, page 44

1 Mira el cuadro y escribe una pregunta para cada dibujo. (AT3/2)

✉ *Reading for information/instructions, Level B*

Reading. Pupils choose an appropriate question from the box for each picture (1–5) and write it down.

Answers

> **1** ¿Quieres ir al club de jóvenes?
> **2** ¿Quieres ir al parque de atracciones?
> **3** ¿Quieres ir a la pista de hielo?
> **4** ¿Quieres ir al cine?
> **5** ¿Quieres ir a la bolera?

2 Empareja las frases con los dibujos. (AT3/2)

✉ *Reading for information/instructions, Level B*

Reading. Pupils match sentences 1–5 with pictures of the different clocks, a–e.

Answers

> **1** d **2** a **3** c **4** e **5** b

3 Lee el diálogo y contesta a las preguntas. (AT3/4) [8T2]

✉ *Reading for information/instructions, Level D*

Reading. Pupils read the conversation and answer questions 1–4.

Answers

> **1** Diego
> **2** He asks her if she wants to go to the disco.
> **3** Tomorrow night.
> **4** At 8.30, at Graciela's house

4 Escribe un diálogo similar para invitar a un(a) amigo/a a salir contigo. (AT4/4) [8S4; 8T2, 6]

✉ *Writing imaginatively, Level C/E*

Writing. Pupils write a similar conversation to invite a friend out.

Hojas de trabajo, Resource and Assessment File, pages 90 and 91

Cards for pairwork featuring places to go and attractions: pupils match the pictures to the correct words.

2 ¿Qué tipo de películas te gustan?
(Pupil's Book pages 78–79)

Main topics
- Saying what type of films you like/dislike
- Saying why you like them

Key Framework objectives
- Word discrimination 9W1 (Launch)
- Unscripted speech 8L5 (Launch)
- Connectives 8W2 (Reinforcement)
- Adding abstract words 8W1 (Reinforcement)
- Youth attitudes to sport/culture 9C3 (Reinforcement)

Other aims
- Pronunciation practice

Grammar
- Adjectives:
aburrido(a)(s)/emocionante(s)/divertido(a)(s)/estúpido(a)(s)/infantil(es), interesante(s)

Key language
¿Qué tipo de películas prefieres?
(No) Me gustan/Prefiero las películas …
románticas   de acción
cómicas   de terror
de ciencia-ficción   de dibujos animados
porque (no) son …

Resources
Cassette C, side 1
CD 3, tracks 4, 5 and 6
Cuaderno A, page 45
OHTs 25–26

Starter 1
Aim: To revise likes/dislikes in different contexts.

Ask pupils to write down three things they like: *me gusta(n)* and three things they dislike: *no me gusta(n)*. This could be written as a 'Haiku' style poem. Encourage a variety of topics – food, subjects, animals, etc. and take feedback.

Suggestion
Introduce this topic using OHTs 25–26.

Realia: bring in adverts for different types of films, stick them on the board and say what they are in Spanish. Can pupils work out what type of films they are?

1a Escucha y repite. Pon atención a la pronunciación. (AT1/2) [8L1]

✖ *Listening for information/instructions, Level A*

Listening. Pupils listen to the recording and repeat the words.

Tapescript
1 Una película romántica
2 Una película cómica
3 Una película de ciencia-ficción
4 Una película de acción
5 Una película de terror
6 Una película de dibujos animados

1b Empareja cada póster con el tipo de película apropiado. (AT3/4)

✖ *Reading for information/instructions, Level B*

Reading. Pupils match the posters and types of film.

Answers

1 e	2 c	3 a	4 b	5 f	6 d

2a Escucha a los jóvenes. ¿Qué tipo de películas prefieren? (1–5) (AT1/3)

✖ *Listening for information/instructions, Level B*

Listening. Pupils listen to the recording and write down what type of film each person prefers.

R Ask pupils to write down the number of the film mentioned for 1–5.

+ Ask pupils to write down what type of films these are in English.

Answers

1 películas de acción   2 películas de terror
3 películas de ciencia-ficción   4 películas cómicas
5 películas de dibujos animados

Tapescript
1 –¿Qué tipo de películas prefieres?
  – Me gustan las películas de acción.
2 –¿Qué tipo de películas prefieres, Juan?
  – Prefiero las películas de terror.
3 –¿Qué tipo de películas prefieres?
  – Prefiero las películas de ciencia-ficción.
4 –¿Qué tipo de películas prefieres?
  – Me gustan mucho las películas cómicas.
5 –¿Qué tipo de películas prefieres, Lola?
  – Me gustan las películas de dibujos animados.

2 ¿Qué tipo de películas te gustan?

módulo 5

2b Haz un sondeo. Pregunta a cinco de tus compañeros/as. Copia y rellena el cuadro. (AT2/2)

✕ *Experiences, feelings, opinions, Level C/E*

Speaking. Pupils copy the grid at the bottom of page 78 and ask five class members what types of films they like. They then fill in information on the grid.

> **Starter 2**
>
> *Aim:* To recap *preferir: prefiero, prefieres.*
>
> Write the following two questions on the board and ask pupils to answer them.
>
> *¿Qué tipo de películas prefieres? Prefiero las películas de …*
>
> *¿Qué tipo de libros prefieres? Prefiero los libros de …*

3a Empareja las palabras. (AT3/1) [8W1]

✕ *Reading for information/instructions, Level A*

Reading. Pupils match the adjectives with the correct meaning in English.

Answers

1 b	**2** c	**3** d	**4** f	**5** a	**6** e

3b Escucha a los jóvenes. ¿Qué tipo de películas prefieren y por qué? (1–4) (AT1/4) [8L3; 9C3]

✕ *Listening for information/instructions, Level D*

Listening. Pupils listen to the recording and write down which films they prefer and why. (1–4)

Answers

1 películas de acción, emocionantes
2 películas de terror, divertidas
3 películas de ciencia-ficción, emocionantes
4 películas cómicas, divertidas

Tapescript

1 – ¿Qué tipo de películas prefieres, Hugo?
– Prefiero las películas de acción porque son emocionantes.
2 – ¿Te gustan las películas de dibujos animados, Pepa?
– No me gustan las películas de dibujos animados. Prefiero las películas de terror.
– ¿Por qué?
– Porque son divertidas.
3 – ¿Qué tipo de películas prefieres, Joaquín?
– Prefiero las películas de ciencia-ficción porque son emocionantes.
4 – ¿Te gustan las películas de acción?
– Sí, me gustan las películas de acción pero me gustan más las películas cómicas porque son divertidas.

3c Con tu compañero/a, pregunta y contesta. (AT2/4) [8W1, 2; 8L4, 5; 9W1]

✕ *Experiences, feelings, opinions, Level C/E*

Speaking. Working in pairs, pupils ask their partner what type of films they prefer and why.

➕ Ask more able pupils to do this without using prompts.

➕ Ask pupils to write these answers down.
(Juan) Prefiere películas de terror porque son emocionantes.
Point out the difference between *¿Por qué?* and *porque.*

4a Lee el correo electrónico y contesta a las preguntas. (AT3/4)

✕ *Reading for information/instructions, Level D*

Reading. Pupils read the e-mail and answer questions 1–7 in English.

Answers

1 science fiction **2** exciting **3** Blade II **4** cartoons
5 childish **6** comedies **7** fun

🖮 **ICT activity**

Ask pupils to compose real e-mails to send to your link school, telling them about the types of films they like and why.

4b Escribe unas frases sobre los tipos de películas que prefieres. (AT4/4) [8W1, 2; 8S6]

✕ *Exchange information/ideas, Level C/E*

Writing. Ask pupils to write down a few sentences about the type of films they prefer and why.

> **Plenary** [8W1]
>
> Ask your class what adjectives were used to describe the different types of films. Take feedback and write these on the board. Discuss strategies for remembering these words.

En casa.

Personal dossier. Ask pupils to up-date their personal dossier. Write a few sentences about the type of films/books they like and why.

Cuaderno A, page 45

1 Mira la información y lee las frases. ¿Quién habla? (AT3/3)

✕ *Reading for information/instructions, Level C*

Reading. Pupils look at the grid and write down who is speaking in 1–6.

Answers

1 Clara	**2** Rafaela	**3** Clara	**4** Valdo
5 Zulema	**6** Esteban		

2 Escribe frases para dar tus opiniones.
(AT4/4) [8W1, 2]

✕ *Exchange information/ideas, Level C/E*

Writing. Pupils choose adjectives from the box and write down their likes and dislikes.

Main topics

- Buying tickets at the cinema
- Asking about film times
- Discussing film categories

Key Framework objectives

- Creative writing 9T5 (Launch)

Other aims

- Looking at the euro

Key language

Dos entradas por favor.
¿Para qué película? Para …

¿Para qué sesión?
Para la sesión de las siete y media.
Aquí tiene.
¿Cuánto es?
Son (once euros).
Apta para …
para mayores de 7 años   todos los públicos
para mayores de 18 años   para mayores de 13 años

Resources

Cassette C, side 1
CD 3, tracks 7 and 8
Cuaderno A, page 46

Starter 1

Aim: To revise time.

Ask pupils to draw six clock faces. Read out six times in Spanish. Pupils draw in the hands on their clock faces to show the correct time.

1 Lee la conversación y contesta a las preguntas. (AT1/4)

✄ *Reading for information/instructions, Level D*

Reading. Pupils read the conversation at the top of page 80 and answer questions 1–4.

Answers

1 2	**2** Bend it like Beckham
3 6.30	**4** 11€

2a Escucha las conversaciones. ¿Cuántas entradas quieren las personas y qué películas quieren ver? (1–3) [8L3]

✄ *Listening for information/instructions, Level D*

Listening. Pupils listen to the recording and write down how many tickets each person wants and which films they want to see.

Answers

1 *'Quiero ser como Beckham'*, 1
2 *'Las dos torres'*, 3
3 *'Camino a la perdición'*, 5

Tapescript

1 – Buenas tardes.
– Buenas tardes. Una entrada, por favor.
– ¿Para qué película?
– Para 'Quiero ser como Beckham'.

– ¿Para qué sesión?
– Para la sesión de las nueve.
– Aquí tiene.
– ¿Cuánto es?
– Son 5,50 euros.
– Gracias.
– De nada.
2 – ¿Qué desea?
– Tres entradas, por favor.
– ¿Para qué película?
– Para 'Las dos torres'.
– ¿Para qué sesión?
– Para la sesión de las ocho y cuarto.
– Aquí tiene.
– ¿Cuánto es?
– Son 16,50 euros.
– Muchas gracias.
– De nada, adiós.
3 – Buenas tardes. Cinco entradas, por favor.
– ¿Para qué película?
– Para 'Camino a la perdición'.
– ¿Para qué sesión?
– Para la sesión de las seis.
– Aquí tiene.
– ¿Cuánto es?
– Son 27,50 euros.
– Tome usted.

2b Escucha otra vez. ¿Para qué sesión quieren las entradas y cuánto cuestan? Copia y rellena la ficha. (1–3) (AT1/4) [8L6]

✄ *Listening for information/instructions, Level D*

Listening. Pupils listen to the recording again and write down the screening time and cost of tickets.

Answers

1 9.00/5,50 euros	**2** 8.15/16,50 euros	**3** 6.00/27,50 euros

You could write down some useful expressions from the recording and ask pupils to put up their hand if they hear one of them. (For example, *¿Cuánto es?*, *Aqui tiene*, *Muchas gracias*, *de nada* etc.)

Tapescript

As for activity 2a

2c Con tu compañero/a, haz un diálogo. (AT2/3)

Speaking and interacting with others, Level D/E

Speaking. Working in pairs, pupils take it in turns to buy a ticket to go and see a film.

Starter 2

Aim: Revising language in this unit.

Ask pupils how to say: 1 tickets 2 For which screening? 3 How much is it? 4 They are … 5 Here you are. 6 You're welcome.

3a Elige una película apropiada para las personas en las fotos. (AT3/3)

Reading for information/instructions, Level C

Reading. Pupils select a suitable film for the people in the photos.

a The Cell = PG13   **c** Evelyn = PG
b Chicago = 12A   **d** The Jungle Book II = U

Answers (*example*)

1 d	**2** a	**3** b	**4** a

3b Escribe unos títulos de películas para cada categoría en **3a**. (AT4/2)

Exchange information/ideas, Level B

Writing. Ask pupils to write down some examples of films for each of the categories in **3a**.

Write down some titles of current popular films/books on the board in Spanish. Can pupils work out what these films/books are? For example '*El Señor de los anillos*' ('Lord of the Rings').

4 En el ordenador, diseña un póster para un cine. Incluye: (AT4/2–4) [8T3; 9T3, 5]

Writing imaginatively, Level B/D

Writing. Pupils design a film poster on the computer and they include the title, what sort of film it is, what category, price of tickets and times of showing.

Suggestion

Pupils could work together in small groups of two or three.

Plenary

Ask someone to tell you how they extract information from a poster/brochure/leaflet that is in Spanish. Ask questions and encourage others to ask questions. Take feedback and write this on the board.

Cuaderno A, page 46

1 Completa el diálogo con la información en la entrada. (AT3/4)

Reading for information/instructions, Level C

Reading. Pupils complete the dialogue with information from the cinema entrance ticket.

Answers

1 dos **2** *El señor de los anillos* **3** (ocho) y cuarto
4 diez euros

2a Lee la información y empareja cada película con la categoría apropiada. (AT3/4) [9T3]

Reading for information/instructions, Level D

Reading. Pupils read the cinema information and match up each film with the appropriate category.

Answers

1 c	**2** a	**3** b

2b Contesta a las preguntas. (AT3/4)

Reading for information/instructions, Level C

Reading. Pupils answer the questions about the text.

Answers

1 Every day **2** January

3 Escribe un diálogo como en **1** y pide entradas para la película que quieres ver en Cine Maremagnum. (AT4/4) [8T6]

Writing imaginatively, Level C/D

Writing. Pupils write a similar dialogue to the one in activity **1** and ask for tickets to go and see a film, as advertised, at the *Cine Maremagnum*.

4 ¡Es genial!

(Pupil's Book pages 82–83)

Main topics

- Describing an event in the present tense

Key Framework objectives

- Building answers from questions 9S4 (Launch)
- Region of the country 9C5 (Reinforcement)
- Verb tenses 8W5 (Reinforcement)
- *Present*, past, future 8S7 (Reinforcement)
- Expression in text 8T2 (Reinforcement)
- Expression in speech 8L6 (Reinforcement)

Other aims

- Writing a letter (postcards)

Key language

Estoy en …
el Museo del Prado   *el Parque Zoológico*
las montañas   *el sur de España*
Estoy con …
mis amigos/mis padres/mi(s) hermano(s)
Hace mal/buen tiempo. Hace sol/calor/frío.
Es …
aburrido   *fenomenal*
divertido   *genial*
estupendo

Resources

Cassette C, side 1
CD 3, track 9
Cuaderno A, page 47

Starter 1 [8W5]

Aim: To revise idioms that take *hacer*.

Ask pupils to think of six weather expressions that start off with *hace*. Give bonus marks to anyone who can give a non-weather phrase e.g. *me hace(n) falta …*

1 Empareja las preguntas con las respuestas apropiadas en la foto. (AT3/4) [8S4; 8T2; 9C5]

✕ *Reading for information/instructions, Level D*

Reading. Ask pupils to match the questions and answers.

Answers

1 d	**2** b	**3** a	**4** c,e	**5** f	**6** g

2 Escucha y empareja las frases con los dibujos. (1–5) (AT1/4) [8W5; 8L6]

✕ *Listening for information/instructions, Level D/E*

Listening. Pupils listen to the recording and match the sentences with the drawings at the bottom of page 82, a–e.

As the recorded speeches are longer than the sentences pupils should be encouraged to listen for the key phrase rather than try to understand everything.

➕ As a follow-up you could play the recording again and ask pupils to tell you any other pieces of information they have understood.

Answers

1 e	**2** b	**3** a	**4** d	**5** c

Tapescript

1 ¡Hola! Estoy en el Parque Zoológico, con mi hermano. Hace buen tiempo. ¡Es genial! Los animales son muy simpáticos.

2 Hoy visitamos el Museo del Prado, en Madrid. El museo es enorme y es muy interesante. Hace mal tiempo pero estoy con mis compañeros del instituto. ¡Es divertido!

3 Aquí hace mucho frío. Estoy con mis padres. Estamos en las montañas. Esquiamos todo el día. ¡Es estupendo!

4 ¡Hola! Estamos en Puerto Banús en el sur de España. Hace mucho sol. Estoy aquí con mis amigos. ¡Es fenomenal! Por la mañana jugamos al fútbol en la playa. Por la tarde descansamos. Por la noche salimos.

5 Estoy en casa. Es aburrido porque todos mis amigos están de vacaciones y no hay nada que hacer. Hace mal tiempo: está nublado y hace frío. Además no puedo ir al cine porque no tengo dinero.

3 Elige un lugar de los dibujos en **2**. Con tu compañero/a, pregunta y contesta. (AT2/3–4) [8S6; 9S4]

✕ *Speaking and interacting with others, Level C/D*

Speaking. Working in pairs, pupils choose one of the drawings in activity 2. They take it in turns to ask and answer questions about where they are.

➕ Turn this activity into a guessing game. Ask pupils to see if they can work out which picture their partner has chosen asking *¿Estás en el museo?* etc.

➕ Encourage pupils to see the relationship between the question forms and the answers in activity **3** (and in activity **1**), showing them how they can build answers from questions.

Aim: To revise *estar.*

Ask pupils to work with a partner. Write the subject pronouns on the board (perhaps just the first three: *yo, tú, él/ella*) and ask them to talk about what they mean in English and to provide the appropriate forms of *estar.*

4 Elige las palabras apropiadas para describir los dibujos. (AT3/2) [8T2]

✂ *Reading for information/instructions, Level C*

Reading. Pupils use 1–4 to write suitable sentences to describe the two pictures.

🐭 ICT activity

Wordprocessing. Working in pairs, provide each pair with a postcard. Ask pupils to write a description on the computer as if they were there.

5 Estás de vacaciones. Utiliza frases de **3** y **4** para escribir una tarjeta postal. [8S6,7]

✂ *Writing to establish/maintain contact, Level C/E*

Writing. Pupils use activities 3 and 4 to help them write a postcard.

✚ Ask pupils to bring in a real postcard (or design one). Write and 'send' it to a real or imaginary friend.

Suggestion

Have a pretend letterbox. Draw names out of a hat and pupils send their postcard to that person.

Plenary [8W5]

Quickly recap the verb *estar* with your class. Use a dice where dots correspond to each subject pronoun, e.g. one dot = *yo*, two dots = *tú*, three dots = *él*, etc. or dice with subject pronouns on them. Pupils work with a partner or a small group and conjugate the verb according to the dot or subject pronoun it lands on.

This is a very important verb and easy to mix up with *ser* at this stage. The more opportunities you get to practise it and reiterate when it is used the better.

Cuaderno A, page 47

1a Lee la tarjeta y contesta a las preguntas. (AT3/4)

✂ *Reading for information/instructions, Level D*

Reading. Pupils read the postcard and answer questions 1–4.

Answers

1 in Seville   **2** For the festival   **3** Busy   **4** Sunny but not very hot

1b Completa la tarjeta con las palabras apropiadas. (AT3/4) [8W5]

✂ *Reading for information/instructions, Level D*

Reading. Pupils complete the postcard with appropriate words from the box.

Answers

1 estoy   **2** hace   **3** hay   **4** es

2 Escribe una tarjeta postal describiendo tus vacaciones, usando las palabras apropiadas de los cuadros. (AT4/3–4) [8S7]

✂ *Writing to establish/maintain contact, Level C/E*

Writing. Pupils write a postcard describing their holiday using words from the grid.

5 ¿Qué hiciste el sábado?

(Pupil's Book pages 84–85)

Main topics

- Using the preterite to describe an event in the past

Key Framework objectives

- Verb tenses (preterite) 8W5 (Reinforcement)
- Present, *past*, future 8S7 (Reinforcement)

Grammar

- Regular *–er* and *–ir* verbs:
  Comer: comí, comiste, comimos
  Salir: salí, saliste, salimos
- Irregular verbs:
  Hacer: hice, hiciste, hicimos
  Ver: vi, viste, vimos

Key language

Salí de casa …
a las cinco y media, a las once, a la una

Fui …
en tren, en autocar, en coche
Vi un partido entre Real Madrid y Valencia.
Comí …
patatas fritas, una hamburguesa con cebolla, un perrito caliente
Bebí …
un café con leche, una Coca-Cola, una naranjada
Vi a Raúl.

Resources

Cassette C, side 1
CD 3, track 10
Cuaderno A, page 48
Grammar, Resource and Assessment File, page 92
OHTs 27–28

Starter 1 [8W5]

Aim: Recaping the preterite in the first person.

Write the following on the board in two columns or prepare an OHT.

1 *compré, visité, fui, me bañé, me alojé*

2 I went, I visited, I stayed, I bathed, I bought

Ask pupils to match the Spanish with the English. Can anyone tell you which verb is irregular? (*fui*). Which groups do the other verbs belong to?

1 Escucha y escribe la letra apropiada. (1–6) (AT1/2) [8W5; 8L3]

✘ *Listening for information/instructions, Level C*

Listening. Explain that pupils are going to learn the preterite of four new verbs. You could write them up and invite pupils to deduce the meaning – the grid on p.84 gives visual clues. The new verbs are *salí, vi, comí, bebí*. Pupils listen to the recording and write down the appropriate letter a, b or c for 1–6.

Answers

1 b	**2** c	**3** b	**4** c	**5** a	**6** b

Tapescript

¿Qué hiciste el sábado?
El sábado fui a un partido de fútbol.
1 – *¿A qué hora saliste de casa?*
   – *Salí de casa a las once.*
2 – *¿Cómo fuiste?*
   – *Fui en coche.*

3 – *¿Qué partido viste?*
   – *Vi un partido entre Barcelona y Betis.*
4 – *¿Qué comiste?*
   – *Comí un perrito caliente.*
5 – *¿Qué bebiste?*
   – *Bebí una Coca-Cola.*
6 – *¿A quién viste?*
   – *Vi a Javier Saviola.*

---

2 Con tu compañero/a, contesta a las preguntas. Elige las respuestas que prefieres (a–c) de **1**. (AT2/5) [8W5; 8S4, 7; 9S4]

✘ *Speaking and interacting with others, Level D*

Speaking. Working in pairs, pupils take it in turns to ask each other the questions about what they did on Saturday. The beginning of each answer is given, pupils must complete the answers by choosing something from **1**, a–c.

Starter 2 [8W5]

Aim: To revise *–ir* verbs in the preterite.

Ask pupils to practise conjugating *salir* and *ir* in the preterite. Use a dice where dots correspond to each subject pronoun, e.g. one dot = *yo*, two dots = *tú*, three dots = *él*, etc. or dice with subject pronouns on them. Pupils work with a partner or a small group and conjugate the verb according to the dot or the subject pronoun it lands on.

3 Escribe seis frases sobre un partido de fútbol o una película. (AT4/5) [8S7]

✠ *Writing imaginatively, Level C/E*

Writing. Pupils write six sentences about a football match or a film they went to see on Saturday (or a different activity entirely!).

◈ ICT activity

'Newsletter' format. Pupils could write an interview with a star about what they did at the weekend.

Plenary [8W5]

Ask a brave pupil to recap the endings to –*ir* verbs in the preterite (and –*ar* verbs if there is time).

Can someone suggest a useful strategy to help learn the preterite of the irregular verbs: *ver* and *hacer*?

Cuaderno A, page 48

1 Lee los textos y escribe S (Selena), R (Rosa), C (Carlos) o V (Verónica) para cada dibujo. (AT3/5) [8S7, 8]

✠ *Reading for information/instructions, Level E*

Reading. Pupils read the text and write the initial of the appropriate person next to pictures 1–7.

Answers

1 S	2 R	3 C	4 R	5 V	6 R	7 C

2 Lee los textos otra vez y rellena el cuadro para Rosa, Carlos y para ti. (AT3/5) [8S7, 8]

✠ *Reading for information/instructions, Level E*

Reading. Pupils read the text again and fill in the grid for Rosa, Carlos and themselves.

Answers

		Rosa	Carlos
No salí de casa.		✔	
Hice mis deberes.		✔	
Vi	un video.	✔	
	la tele.		
Jugué con la Playstation.		✔	
Salí con	un(a) amigo/a.		✔
	mis padres.		
Fui	de excursión al campo.		✔
	al cine.		
	a un partido de fútbol.		
Leí	un libro.	✔	
	el periódico.		
	una revista.		

3 Escribe sobre lo que hiciste el fin de semana pasado. (AT4/5) [8S7]

✠ *Exchange information/ideas, Level C/E*

Writing. Pupils write about what they did last weekend.

Grammar, Resource and Assessment File, page 92 (More about the preterite tense)

1

Pupils identify the verbs in the sentences.

Answers

a jugué
b salí
c compré
d fui/pasé
e vi
f comí/bebí

2

Pupils fill in the blanks in a grid to translate various verbs into English. They then put them into the preterite (1st person singular) with their corresponding meanings.

Infinitive	Meaning	Preterite	Meaning
comer	*to eat*	comí	I ate
salir	to go out	*salí*	*I went out*
beber	*to drink*	bebí	I drank
visitar	*to visit*	visité	I visited
comprar	to buy	*compré*	I bought
ver	to see	vi	*I saw*
ir	*to go*	fui	*I went*

3

Pupils use what they know about the verbs to decide which is the odd one out and say why.

Answers

ir – the preterite form is different to the infinitive and is always followed by *a*.

4

Pupils write their own rules to help them remember the preterite endings for –*er*, –*ar* and –*ir* verbs, as well as irregular verbs.

Resumen y Prepárate

(Pupil's Book pages 86–87)

Resumen

This is a checklist of language covered in Module 5. There is a comprehensive Resumen list for Module 5 in the Pupil's Book (page 86) and a Resumen test sheet in Cuaderno A (page 52)

Key Framework objectives

● Present, past, future 8S7 (Reinforcement)

Prepárate

A revision test to give practice for the test itself at the end of the module.

Resources

Cassette C, side 1
CD 3, tracks 11 and 12
Cuaderno A, pages 49, 50, 51 and 52
Resumen, Resource and Assessment File, page 96
Skills, Resource and Assessment File, page 94

---

1 ¿Qué tipo de películas les gustan? Escucha y elige el dibujo apropiado para cada diálogo. (1–4) (AT1/3) [8L3]

✄ *Listening for information/instructions, Level D*

Listening. Pupils listen to the recording and choose the appropriate drawing for each dialogue.

Answers

1 b	2 c	3 d	4 a

Tapescript

1 – ¿Qué tipo de películas prefieres, Lara?
– Me gustan las películas de acción porque son emocionantes.
2 – ¿Qué tipo de películas te gustan, Alejandro?
– Me gustan las películas de ciencia-ficción. Son muy interesantes.
3 – ¿Te gustan las películas románticas, Miriam?
– No, no me gustan las películas románticas. Me gustan las películas de terror.
4 – ¿Te gustan las películas de terror, Miguel?
– No, no me gustan. ¡Prefiero los dibujos animados!

2a Escucha el diálogo y elige el dibujo apropiado (a–c) para cada frase. (1–4) (AT1/3) [8L3]

✄ *Listening for information/instructions, Level D*

Listening. Pupils listen to the recording and choose an appropriate drawing, a–c, for each sentence.

Answers

1 c	2 c	3 c	4 a

Tapescript

1 – ¡Hola , Pablo! ¿Quieres ir al parque de atracciones?
– ¿Cuándo?
2 – El domingo.
– ¡Buena idea! ¿A qué hora quedamos?
3 – A las diez y media.
– Vale. ¿Dónde quedamos?
4 – En la plaza.
– Bueno.

– Adiós.
– Adiós, hasta luego.

2b Con tu compañero/a, haz un diálogo similar. Utiliza los dibujos en **2a**. (AT2/3–4)

✄ *Speaking and interacting with others, Level D/E*

Speaking. Working in pairs, pupils have a similar dialogue to that in **2a**.

3a Copia y completa las frases con las palabras apropiadas. (AT3/5) [8S7]

✄ *Reading for information/instructions, Level D*

Reading. Pupils complete Alberto's letter by choosing suitable words to fill in the gaps.

Answers

1 fui	2 Fui	3 Salí	4 Fui	5 Comí	6 Bebí

3b Escribe cuatro frases en español para contestar a la pregunta: ¿Y tú? ¿Qué hiciste el sábado? (AT4/5)

✄ *Exchange information/ideas, Level C/E*

Writing. Pupils write down four sentences about what they did on Saturday.

Cuaderno A, page 49

Repaso

1 Completa el crucigrama. (AT3/4)

✄ *Reading for pleasure*

Reading. Pupils do the crossword.

Answers

¹E		²L		³N	⁴C	A	⁵L	O	⁶R	
⁷S	Á	⁸B	A	⁹D	O		E		I	
		O		O	A		Í		C	
¹⁰P	E	L	Í	C	U	¹¹L	A		A	
	E		E		L					
¹²H	O	R	A		E		¹³H	o	¹⁴H	
A		A			¹⁵V	E	R	A	N	O
Y		¹⁶N	A	D	É		C		O	
							E		L	
									A	

Cuaderno A, page 50

Gramática 1

1 Complete the grid with the correct forms of each adjective.

⚑ *Knowing about language*

Writing. Pupils complete the grid with adjectives from the box.

Answers

masculine singular	feminine singular	masculine plural	feminine plural	
aburrido	aburrida	aburridos	aburridas	*boring*
divertido	divertida	divertidos	divertidas	*fun*
romántico	romántica	románticos	románticas	*romantic*
estúpido	estúpida	estúpidos	estúpidas	*silly*
emocionante	emocionante	emocionantes	emocionantes	*exciting*
inteligente	inteligente	inteligentes	inteligentes	*intelligent*
interesante	interesante	interesantes	interesantes	*interesting*
infantil	infantil	infantiles	infantiles	*childish*

2a Complete the sentences with the correct form of the adjective.

⚑ *Knowing about language*

Writing. Pupils complete the sentences with the correct form of the adjectives given, using the help box.

Answers

1 infantiles **2** aburridas **3** interesante

2b Complete the sentences about yourself with the correct form of the adjective, using the grid in **1**. Delete the alternatives as appropriate.

⚑ *Knowing about language*

Writing. Pupils complete the sentences about themselves with the correct form of adjectives.

Cuaderno A, page 51

Gramática 2

1 Complete the postcards with the correct words.

⚑ *Knowing about language*

Reading. Pupils complete the postcards with the correct verbs taken from the box.

Answers

Postcard 1: **Estoy** de vacaciones en España. Aquí hace buen tiempo. Hace sol y **hace** calor. El hotel **es** estupendo. **Está** cerca de la playa. Mañana **hay** una fiesta. Se llama la Tomatina. Los chicos **son** muy guapos y muy simpáticos.

Postcard 2: Gracias por tu tarjeta de España. **Estoy** de vacaciones en Gales. Hace buen tiempo pero no **hace** calor. El camping **es** divertido. Hay muchos jóvenes aquí, ¡pero no **hay** chicos guapos!

2 Complete the sentences with the correct verbs.

⚑ *Knowing about language*

Reading. Pupils complete the sentences with the correct verbs taken from the box.

Answers

1 Salí **2** Vi **3** Fui **4** Leí **5** Bebí **6** Comí **7** Vi **8** Hice

Skills, Resource and Assessment File, page 94 (Building sentences)

1

Answers

¿Cuándo?	When?
¿Dónde?	Where?
¿Qué tal?	What like?
¿Qué?	*What?*
¿Cómo?	How?
¿Con quién?	Who with?

2

Answers

a ¿Cuándo?
b ¿Qué tal?
c ¿Qué?
d ¿Con quién?
e ¿Dónde?

3

Cuándo?	¿Dónde?	¿Qué tal?	¿Qué?	¿Cómo?	¿Con quién?
el lunes	en el salón	era genial	comí	en coche	mis amigos
por la tarde	a la playa	me divertí	jugué	en autobús	mi hermano
por la mañana	al parque temático	era estupendo	nadé	en bici	mis padres
esta noche	al cine	era aburrido	salí	a pie	mis abuelos

4

Pupils add two more examples to each of the columns in 3.

5

Pupils add to the sentences using phrases from the grid in 3.

6

Pupils now write sentences of their own trying to answer as many sentences from the grid headings in 3 as they can.

6 ¡Extra! ¿Qué tal el fin de semana? (Pupil's Book pages 88–89)

Main topics

This is an optional extension unit which revises and extends some of the key language of the module. It introduces the imperfect tense to describe the weather and what something was like in the past.

Key Framework objectives

- Verb tenses (preterite) 8W5 (Reinforcement)
- Question types 8S4 (Reinforcement)
- Present, past, future 8S7 (Reinforcement)

Key language

Hacía …
sol   *viento*
calor   *buen/mal tiempo*
frío
Había mucha gente
Era fenomenal
¡Era un desastre!

Resources

Cassette C, side 1
CD 3, track 13

Starter 1 [8W5]

Aim: Conjugating verbs in the preterite.

Ask pupils to work with a partner and write out the paradigms for the following verbs: *comer, visitar, ir.*

Suggestion

To familiarise pupils with the texts get them to do a scavenger hunt. For example, ask them to find **1** 5 places referred to **2** 3 weather expressions **3** 2 modes of transport and **4** 1 adjective. Set a time limit for this activity.

1a Escucha y lee. ¿Adónde fueron los chicos? Empareja los jóvenes con los textos apropiados. [8S7]

Listening/Reading. Pupils listen to the recording and match the people in 1–5 with the appropriate texts.

Answers

1 c   2 d   3 a   4 b   5 e

Tapescript

1 – ¡Hola, Cristina! ¿Qué tal el fin de semana?
– *El domingo visité a mis abuelos. Había mucha gente: mis padres, mis tíos y mis primos. Comimos en un restaurante porque fue el cumpleaños de mi abuela.*
2 – ¡Hola, Miguel! ¿Qué hiciste el fin de semana?
– *Salimos de casa el viernes por la noche y llegamos al camping bastante tarde. El sábado empezó a llover y hacía mucho viento. ¡Fue un desastre!*
3 – Tamara, ¿Qué tal tu fin de semana? ¿Lo pasaste bien?
– *Lo pasé muy bien. El sábado fui a un zoo con tres amigos. Fuimos en autocar. Por la mañana hacía buen tiempo. Mis animales favoritos son los elefantes. ¡Fue genial!*
4 – ¿Y Daniel? ¿Qué hiciste?
– *El fin de semana fui a Londres con mis padres. Viajamos en tren. Primero fuimos de compras en Covent Garden. Hacía sol y había mucha gente. Por la tarde fuimos al río Tamesis y vimos el museo del Tate Modern.*

5 – ¿Qué tal tu fin de semana, Lorena? ¿Qué hiciste?
– *El domingo por la tarde fui al cine. Vi 'Quiero ser como Beckham'. Es una película estupenda. Y además comí un cartón enorme de palomitas de maíz.*

1b Lee los textos (a–e) otra vez. (AT3/5) [8S7]

Reading for information/instructions, Level E

Reading. Pupils look at the text again and answer 1–5 in English.

Answers

1 weather was good, saw her favourite animal
2 lots of people, sunny
3 Cristina
4 disaster/bad weather (wind and rain)
5 yes/fantastic film

2 Con tu compañero/a, pregunta y contesta. Utiliza información de los textos (a–e) o información personal. (AT2/5) [8S4]

Speaking and interacting with others, Level D/E

Speaking. Working in pairs, pupils ask and answer the questions using either information from the text or personal information. They could write up their replies.

Plenary [8S7]

Ask pupils to find the following in the text:

1 I had a great time (*lo pasé muy bien*)   **2** I went (*fui*)   **3** we went (*fuimos*)   **4** we ate in a restaurant (*comimos en un restaurante*)   **5** It was sunny (*hacía sol*)   **6** It was a disaster (*era un desastre*)   **7** There were a lot of people (*había mucha gente*)

módulo 5 — Te toca a ti

(Pupil's Book pages 116–117)

- Self-access reading and writing at two levels.

Key Framework objectives

- Word, phrase, clause sequencing 8S1
- Present, past, future 8S7 (Reinforcement)
- Text as model 8T6 (Reinforcement)

A Reinforcement

1 Elige las frases para los dibujos. (AT3/2)

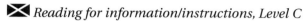 *Reading for information/instructions, Level C*

Reading. Pupils match the sentences with the appropriate drawings.

Answers

1 b	2 d	3 e	4 c	5 a	6 f	7 h	8 g

2 Pon la conversación en el orden correcto. (AT3/4) [8S1]

Reading for information/instructions, Level D

Reading. Pupils put the conversation into the correct order.

Answers

1 d	2 c	3 b	4 a

3 Escribe un diálogo como en **2**. (AT4/4) [8S1]

Writing imaginatively, Level C/E

Writing. Pupils use the previous exercise as a model to write out a similar conversation

4 Elige una frase para cada dibujo. (AT3/3)

Reading for information/instructions, Level C

Reading. Pupils choose a sentence to go with each drawing.

Answers

a 4	b 1	c 6	d 5	e 3	f 2

B Extension

1 Lee el diario de Juan y contesta a las preguntas. (AT3/5) [8S7]

Reading for information/instructions, Level E

Reading. Pupils read Juan's diary and answer questions 1–5 in English.

Answers

1 cinema
2 yes, loves action films (saw the James Bond film!)
3 the afternoon, ate out (steak and chips!)
4 read a newspaper and a magazine
5 holiday

2 Escribe tu diario para el fin de semana pasado. (AT4/5) [8S7; 8T6]

Writing imaginatively, Level D/E

Writing. Pupils use Juan's diary as a model to write their own diary for last week end.

módulo 6

La salud

(Pupil's Book pages 92–107)

Unit	Key Framework objectives	PoS	Key language and Grammar
1 ¿Qué te duele? (pp. 92–93) Saying what is wrong with you	8W4 Word endings [R] 8C4 Poems, jokes, songs [R]	5g listening/ reading for enjoyment	*Doler* Pronouns: *me* and *te* *Me duele, te duele* *Me duelen, te duelen* *Me duele (el estómago), me duelen (los pies).*
2 ¿Qué te pasa? (pp. 94–95) Saying what is wrong with you Asking others what is wrong with them	8S6 Substituting and adding [R] 8L4 Extending sentences [R]	2a listen for gist and detail	Illnesses using *tener*: *¿Qué te pasa?* *Tengo (fiebre).*
3 En la farmacia (pp. 96–97) Asking for things at the chemist Understanding the pharmacist's recommendations	9L6 Formality of language [L] 8S3 Modal verbs [R]	1a sounds and writing 2a listen for gist and detail 2b pronunciation/ intonation 2c ask and answer questions 2i report main points 5e range of resources	*Deber: debes* *Ser: es, son* Demonstrative adjectives: *este, esta, estas* Adjectives: *bueno/a(s), fuerte(s), grande(s), pequeño/a(s)* *¿Tiene algo para (la diarrea)?* *Este (jarabe) es (bueno).* *Estas (aspirinas) son (buenas).* *Deme un tubo (grande).*
4 Hace dos años que estudio español (pp. 98–99) Talking about how long you've been doing something	8L2 Media listening skills [L] 8W8 Non-literal meanings [R] 8S1 Sequencing [R] 8S7 Present, past, future [R] 8C3 Daily life and young people [R]	5d respond to different types of language 5e range of resources	*Hace … que* *¿Cuánto tiempo hace que (juegas al fútbol)?* *Hace (un mes/dos años) que (juego al fútbol)*
5 No hay que comer chocolate todos los días (pp. 100–101) Talking about a healthy lifestyle Saying what you should/ shouldn't do	8S2 Connectives in extended sentences [R] 8S3 Modal verbs [R] 8S7 Present, past, *future* [R] 8L2 Media listening skills	4d consider experiences in other countries 5e range of resources	*(No) Hay que* + verb *(No) Tienes que* + verb Immediate future: *voy a* + infinitive *Hay que (beber 2 litros de agua al día).* *Tienes que (hacer deporte tres veces a la semana).*

Unit	Key Framework objectives	PoS	Key language and Grammar
Resumen y Prepárate (pp. 102–103) Pupil's checklist and practice test			
6 ¡Extra! Entrevista con una deportista (pp. 88–89) Optional unit: using '*Hay que ...*' and the immediate future	8S7 Present, past, future [R] 8S8 Using high-frequency words [R] 8T3 Language and text types [R] 8L2 Media listening skills [R]	4a working with authentic materials	
Te toca a ti (pp.118–119) Self-access reading and writing at two levels			

Main topics

- Saying what is wrong with you

Key Framework objectives

- Word endings 8W4 (Reinforcement)
- Poems, jokes, songs 8C4 (Reinforcement)

Grammar

- Pronouns: *me* and *te*
- *Doler*
  Me duele, te duele
  Me duelen, te duelen

Key language

Me duele(n) …
los pies   los oídos

la cabeza	*las piernas*
la mano	*la espalda*
la garganta	*las muelas*
los brazos	*el estómago*

Resources

Cassette C, side 1
CD 3, tracks 14, 15, 16 and 17
Cuaderno A, page 53
Starter 2, Resource and Assessment File, page 111
Hojas de trabajo, Resource and Assessment File, pages 114 and 115 (*el brazo, las muelas, la mano, el oído, el pie, la cabeza, la garganta, la pierna, la espalda, el estómago*)
Grammar, Resource and Assessment File, page 116
OHTs 31, 32

Starter 1 [8W4]

Aim: To introduce parts of the body and to revise the definite article: *el, la, los, las*

Use OHTs 31 and 32. Blank out the definite article and ask pupils to predict what the article is, using the endings of the nouns as clues. Note the rogue *la mano*.

If you do not have the OHTs, write the parts of the body on the board (taken from page 92) and do the same as above.

1a Empareja las partes del cuerpo con los nombres. (AT3/1)

✕ *Reading for information/instructions, Level A*

Reading. Pupils match the parts of the body with their names.

Answers

As tapescript for **1b**

1b Escucha y comprueba tus respuestas.

✕ *Listening for information/instructions, Level A*

Listening. Pupils listen to the recording and check their answers.

Tapescript

a *las muelas*
b *el estómago*
c *la espalda*
d *las piernas*
e *los pies*
f *los brazos*
g *las manos*

h *la garganta*
i *los oídos*
j *la cabeza*

2a Lee y escucha la canción. ¿Qué partes del cuerpo no se mencionan? (AT3/3) [8C4]

✕ *Listening for enjoyment*

Listening. Pupils listen to the recording and write down the parts of the body that are not mentioned in the song.

Answers

La garganta, los oídos, las muelas, el estómago

Tapescript

Mueve tu cuerpo
Muévete, muévete.
Mueve tu cuerpo,
Muévete, muévete.
(refrán)

Mueve la cabeza
Arriba, abajo.
Mueve la espalda
A la derecha, a la izquierda
Mueve las piernas
Para adelante, para atrás
Mueve los pies.

Mueve las manos
Arriba, abajo.
Mueve las rodillas
Para adelante, para atrás
Mueve los brazos
El derecho, el izquierdo
Mueve los pies.

You may want to teach *las rodillas* (knees) before playing the song.

117

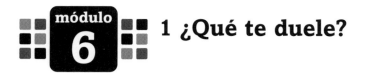

💿 **ICT activity**

Fun with texts. Using *Text salad*, input the lines from the song and jumble them up. Pupils listen to the song again and put them in the correct order.

Or, using *Copywrite hard*, blank out the parts of the body. Pupils listen to the song and using the same program fill in the gaps.

2b Escucha otra vez y mueve las partes del cuerpo como indica la canción. (AT1/4) [8C4]

✠ *Listening for enjoyment*

Listening. Pupils listen to the song again and move the parts of their body the song tells them to.

Tapescript

As for activity 2a.

2c Dile a tu compañero/a, que mueva varias partes del cuerpo. (AT2/2)

✠ *Speaking to convey information, Level C*

Speaking. Working in pairs, pupils take it in turns to follow their partner's instructions.

➕ Play 'Simon says' with your class or in small groups.

Song: Ask pupils to make up their own version of 'Head, shoulders, knees and toes': *la cabeza, (la espalda), las rodillas y los pies.*

Starter 2

Aim: Practising vocabulary: parts of the body.

Using *Resource and Assessment File*, page 111 give some of the parts of the body as anagrams. Set a time limit and see who can finish first.

1 spie (*pies*)	5 slamue (*muelas*)
2 moan (*mano*)	6 soodí (*oídos*)
3 snapier (*piernas*)	7 óotesgam (*estómago*)
4 pladsea (*espalda*)	8 beazac (*cabeza*)

3a ¿Qué les duele a estas personas? Escucha y elige el dibujo apropiado. (1–6) (AT1/2) [8L3]

✠ *Listening for information/instructions, Level B*

Listening. Pupils listen to the recording and choose the appropriate picture.

Answers

1 f	2 d	3 c	4 b	5 a	6 e

Tapescript

1 – ¿Qué te duele?
– Me duelen los brazos.

2 – ¡Ay!
– ¿Qué te duele?
– Me duele el estómago.
3 – ¿Qué te duele?
– Me duelen los pies.
4 – ¿Qué te duele?
– Me duele mucho la cabeza.
5 – ¿Qué te duele?
– Me duele la garganta.
6 – ¿Qué te duele?
– Me duelen las muelas.

3b Empareja las frases con los dibujos en **3a**. (AT3/2)

✠ *Reading for information/instructions, Level B*

Reading. Pupils match the sentences with the drawings.

Answers

1 b	2 a	3 f	4 c	5 d	6 e

3c Con tu compañero/a, haz conversaciones con tres de las personas en **3a**. (AT2/2) [9W4]

✠ *Speaking and interacting with others, Level C/D*

Speaking. Working in pairs, pupils choose three of the people in 3a to have a conversation with, asking them what is wrong.

🎭 **Drama.** Mime. Divide the class into two teams. Invite volunteers up and give them an illness to mime. The team to guess first gets a point.

3d Escribe una frase para cada dibujo. (AT4/2) [9W4]

✠ *Exchange information/ideas, Level C*

Writing. Pupils write a sentence for drawings 1–4.

Plenary

Quick fire questions: How would pupils say the following:

I have a headache, I have a stomachache, My feet ache, I have a sore throat.

Cuaderno A, page 53

1 Lee los globos y rellena el cuadro. (AT3/3)

✠ *Reading for information/instructions, Level D*

Reading. Pupils read the speech bubbles and fill in the grid.

Answers

	1 Marián	2 Ramón	3 Laura	4 Martín
1	✔		✔	
2			✔	
3	✔			
4			✔	
5		✔		
6		✔		
7			✔	
8			✔	✔
9		✔		✔
10				
11		✔		✔

2 ¿Qué les duele? Escribe una frase para cada persona. (AT4/2) [9W4]

✉ *Exchange information/ideas, Level C*

Writing. Practising '*doler*': Pupils look at the pictures and write down what is wrong with each person, 1–7.

Answers

1 Me duelen los pies.   **2** Me duele la garganta. **3** Me duele la espalda.   **4** Me duele el estómago. **5** Me duelen las muelas.   **6** Me duelen los brazos. **7** Me duelen los oídos.

Hojas de trabajo, Resource and Assessment File, pages 114 and 115

Cards for pairwork featuring parts of the body and ailments: pupils match the pictures to the correct words.

Grammar, Resource and Assessment File, page 116

1

Saying what hurts

Pupils use the correct form of the verb *doler* (*duele/ duelen*) to make a sentence with the ailments given.

Answers

a *Me duele la cabeza.*   **b** Me duelen los pies. **c** Me duelen las muelas.   **d** Me duele la garganta. **e** Me duele el estómago.   **f** Me duelen los oídos.

Some key verbs

2

Pupils choose the correct verbs from the box to complete the sentences.

Answers

a Tus notas del cole son malas. Tienes que estudiar más. **b** No me gusta mi nuevo colegio porque hay que llevar uniforme. **c** Para coger el autobús debes salir de casa a las ocho. **d** Si tienes dolor de cabeza hay que tomar una aspirina. **e** Para seguir una dieta sana tienes que comer mucha fruta y verduras. **f** Si quieres estar en forma debes hacer ejercicio.

3

Pupils translate the instructions left by Ricardo's mother into English.

Answers

a Wash the dishes	**b** Call his grandmother
c Do his homework	**d** Tidy his room

módulo 6

2 ¿Qué te pasa?

(Pupil's Book pages 94–95)

Main topics

● Saying what is wrong with you
● Asking others what is wrong with them

Key Framework objectives

● Substituting and adding 8S6 (Reinforcement)
● Extending sentences 8L4

Grammar

● Illnesses using *tener*:
tengo tos, tiene gripe

Key language

¿Qué te pasa?
Tengo …

fiebre   *una picadura*
una insolación   *dolor de cabeza*
tos   *gripe*
diarrea   *dolor de estómago*
catarro   *dolor de garganta*

Resources

Cassette C, side 1
CD 3, tracks 18, 19 and 20
Cuaderno A, page 54
Hojas de trabajo, Resource and Assessment File,
pages 114 and 115 (*tengo fiebre, tengo una picadura,
tengo una insolación, tengo catarro*)
Flashcards 43–48
OHTs 31, 32

Starter 1 [8W5]

Aim: Revising *tener* – using it in a different contexts.

Ask the following questions. *¿Cuántos hermanos
tienes? ¿Qué animales tienes en casa? ¿Qué tienes
en tu dormitorio?*

1a Escucha y escribe los dibujos en el orden
correcto. (1–10) (AT1/2) [8L3]

✖ *Listening for information/instructions, Level B*

Listening. Ask pupils to listen to the recording and
write down the drawings in the correct order.

Answers

1 b	2 h	3 c	4 e	5 f	6 d	7 a	8 g	9 j	10 i

Tapescript

1 – *¿Qué te pasa?*
    – *Tengo tos.*
2 – *¿Qué te pasa?*
    – *Tengo dolor de cabeza.*
3 – *¿Qué te pasa?*
    – *Tengo fiebre.*
4 – *¿Qué te pasa?*
    – *Tengo catarro.*
5 – *¿Qué te pasa?*
    – *Tengo diarrea.*
6 – *¿Qué te pasa?*
    – *Tengo una picadura.*
7 – *¿Qué te pasa?*
    – *Tengo una insolación.*
8 – *¿Qué te pasa?*
    – *Tengo gripe.*
9 – *¿Qué te pasa?*
    – *Tengo dolor de garganta.*
10 – *¿Qué te pasa?*
    – *Tengo dolor de estómago.*

1b Con tu compañero/a, pregunta y contesta.
(AT2/2) [8S6]

✖ *Speaking and interacting with others, Level C/D*

Speaking. Working in pairs, pupils take it in turns to
ask their partner what is wrong with them.

Starter 2 [8W5]

Aim: To practise illnesses with the verb *tener*.

Ask pupils to draw or write three illnesses on a
piece of paper and fold it so their partner can't see
what they are. The aim of the game is to be the first
one to guess their partner's illnesses.

2a Escucha y empareja las conversaciones con
los dibujos. (1–5) (AT1/3) [8L3]

✖ *Listening for information/instructions, Level C*

Listening. Pupils listen to the recording and match
the conversations with the drawings.

Answers

1 c	2 b	3 e	4 a	5 d

Tapescript

1 – *¡Mamá! No puedo ir al instituto.*
    – *¿Por qué? ¿Qué te pasa?*
    – *Tengo dolor de estómago y tengo diarrea.*
    – *¡Pues a la cama inmediatamente!*
2 – *¿Qué le pasa?*
    – *Fui a la playa y ahora tengo una insolación.*
    – *¡Vaya!*
    – *Tengo fiebre y dolor de cabeza.*
3 – *¡Ay!*
    – *¿Qué te pasa?*
    – *Tengo una picadura.*
    – *¿Una picadura? ¿Dónde?*
    – *En el brazo.*

4 – ¿Qué tal?
– Mal, muy mal.
– ¿Qué te pasa?
– Tengo catarro. Tengo tos y dolor de garganta.
5 – ¡Ay!
– ¿Qué te pasa?
– Tengo gripe. Tengo fiebre y dolor de cabeza.

2b Escucha otra vez. ¿Qué les pasa y qué síntomas tienen las personas? (AT1/3) [8L3]

✳ *Listening for information/instructions, Level C*

Listening. Pupils listen to the recording again and write down what is wrong with each person as well as their symptoms.

Answers

1 stomach ache, diarrhoea **2** sunburn, fever, headache
3 insect bite (no symptoms mentioned)
4 cold, cough, sore throat **5** flu, fever, headache

Tapescript

*As for activity **2a***

2c Con tu compañero/a, haz el papel de las personas en dos de los dibujos en **2a**. (AT2/3) [8S6; 8L4]

✳ *Speaking and interacting with others, Level C*

Speaking. Working in pairs, pupils role-play two of the conversations from **2a**.

Suggestion

Encourage pupils to put some 'oomph' into this rather than acting like a couple of paper dolls! Ask someone from the drama department if they could spare some time to help or give you some tips on role-play.

3a Escribe las palabras correctas para cada dibujo. (AT4/2) [8S6]

✳ *Exchange information/ideas, Level B*

Writing. Pupils fill in the gaps in the two sick notes.

Answers

1 catarro **2** tos **3** garganta **4** estómago
5 diarrea **6** (tiene) dolor de cabeza.

➕ Ask pupils to write their own sick note using one of the above as a template.

👄 **ICT activity**

Recording (or simply done as a role-play). Working in pairs, pupils play the roles of the parent of a sick child and the school secretary. The parent phones up the school to say what is wrong with child. The school secretary answers, very sympathetic and takes notes of symptoms to tell the teacher. Play these recordings back to the class.

3b Lee las notas en **3a** otra vez. ¿Verdad (✓) o mentira (✗)? (AT3/3)

✳ *Reading for information/instructions, Level D*

Reading. Pupils note true (✓) or false (✗) for 1–6.

Answers

1 ✓ 2 ✗ 3 ✓ 4 ✗ 5 ✓ 6 ✗

➕ Ask pupils to correct the answers that are false.

🎭 **Drama** Circular memory game. Pupils sit in a circle with one person in the middle who pretends to be the doctor. They must ask the question *¿Qué te pasa?* The pupils say what is wrong with them and try to remember previous answers. If they can't they must swap seats with the 'doctor' in the middle.

Plenary [8W5]

See who can remember how to conjugate *tener* (*yo, tú, él/ella*).

How do you say: I have a headache, I have a cough, I have a sore throat, he has an insect bite, she has sunburn?

If time allows, discuss strategies for remembering the new vocabulary and how to spell it correctly.

Cuaderno A, page 54

1 Escribe las frases apropiadas para cada dibujo. (AT3/2)

✳ *Reading for information/instructions, Level B*

Reading. Pupils choose an appropriate speech bubble and write down what is wrong with each person for pictures 1–4.

Answers

1 Tengo gripe, Tengo tos, Tengo fiebre
2 Me duele la pierna
3 Me duele la mano, Tengo una picadura
4 Tengo dolor de cabeza, Tengo una insolación, Me duele la espalda

2 Estás enfermo/a. Escribe una carta a un(a) amigo/a para decir que no puedes ir a su fiesta. (AT4/2–4) [8T5, 7; 9W4]

✳ *Writing to establish/maintain contact, Level C/E*

Writing. Pupils write a letter to a friend saying that they are ill and cannot go to their party.

3 En la farmacia

(Pupil's Book pages 96–97)

Main topics

- Asking for things at the chemist
- Understanding a pharmacist's recommendations

Key Framework objectives

- Formality of language 9L6 (Launch)
- Modal verbs 8S3 (Reinforcement)

Other aims

- Pronunciation practice

Grammar

- *Deber: debes ponerte una tirita, debes tomar unas pastillas, debes ir a la cama*
- *Ser: es, son*
- Demonstrative adjectives: *este jarabe, esta pomada, estas aspirinas*
- Adjectives: *bueno/a(s), fuerte(s), grande(s), pequeño/a(s)*

Key language

¿Tiene algo para (la diarrea)?
Este jarabe es …
Esta pomada es …
Estas aspirinas son …
Deme un tubo (grande).
una caja de aspirinas
una caja de pastillas
una botella de jarabe para la tos
un tubo de pomada
un paquete de tiritas
un tubo de crema antiséptica

Resources

Cassette C, side 1
CD 3, tracks 21, 22, 23 and 24
Cuaderno A, page 55
Starter 2, Resource and Assessment File, page 111
OHTS 31, 32

Starter 1 [8W5]

Aim: To practise illnesses using *tener.*

Write the subject pronouns on the board, or call them out. Pupils fill in the appropriate form of *tener* for each one: *yo tengo, tú tienes, él tiene, ella tiene …*

Mime out four illnesses (or write these on the board in English if you prefer).

Pupils write down or say what is wrong with you, or them if you wish to practise *tienes: tienes dolor de cabeza, tienes dolor de muelas, tienes dolor de estómago.*

1a Escucha y repite. Pon atención a la pronunciación. (AT1/1) [8L1]

✖ *Listening for information/instructions, Level B*

Listening. Pupils listen to the recording and repeat the words.

Tapescript

1 *Una caja de aspirinas.*
2 *Una caja de pastillas para la tos.*
3 *Una botella de jarabe para la tos.*
4 *Un paquete de tiritas.*
5 *Un tubo de pomada.*
6 *Un tubo de crema antiséptica.*

➕ Get pupils to listen to the recording again and write down what they think each item is in English.

1b Escucha las conversaciones. ¿Qué les pasa a estas personas? ¿Qué recomienda la farmacéutica? (1–5) (AT1/4) [8L3; 9L6]

✖ *Listening for information/instructions, Level D*

Listening. Pupils listen to the recording and write down what is wrong with each person and what treatment the pharmacist recommends.

Answers

1 tos, jarabe	**2** dolor de cabeza, aspirinas		
3 picadura, crema	**4** diarrea, pastillas		
5 insolación, pomada			

Tapescript

1 – *¿Tiene algo para la tos?*
   – *Este jarabe es muy bueno.*
   – *Deme una botella de jarabe entonces.*
   – *¿Grande o pequeña?*
   – *Pequeña, por favor.*
   – *Tome usted.*
2 – *¿Tiene algo para el dolor de cabeza?*
   – *Estas aspirinas son bastante fuertes.*
   – *Deme una caja, por favor.*
   – *¿Grande o pequeña?*
   – *Grande, por favor.*
   – *Tome usted, una caja de aspirinas.*
   – *Gracias.*
3 – *¿Tiene algo para las picaduras?*
   – *Esta crema es muy buena.*
   – *Pues deme un tubo de crema.*
   – *¿Grande o pequeño?*
   – *Pequeño, por favor.*
   – *Aquí tiene.*

4 – ¿Tiene algo para la diarrea?
– Estas pastillas son muy buenas.
– Deme una caja.
– ¿Grande o pequeña?
– Grande, por favor.
– Tome, una caja grande.
5 – ¿Tiene algo para la insolación?
– Esta pomada es muy buena.
– Muy bien, deme un tubo de pomada, por favor.
– ¿Grande o pequeño?
– Pequeño, por favor.
– Tome usted, un tubo pequeño.

1c Escucha otra vez. ¿Las personas compran algo grande o pequeño? (AT1/4) [8L3; 9L6]

✉ *Listening for information/instructions, Level D*

Listening. Pupils listen to the recording again. This time they write down whether the item they buy is big or small.

Answers

1 pequeña	**2** grande	**3** pequeño	**4** grande	**5** pequeño

Tapescript

As for activity **1b**

Starter 2 [8S1]

Aim: Vocabulary practice.

Write the following on the board or use *Resource and Assessment File*, page 111 and ask pupils to unscramble them:

1 *tiritas de caja una* (*una caja de tiritas*)
2 *aspirinas de una caja* (*una caja de aspirinas*)
3 *tubo un de antiséptica crema* (*un tubo de crema antiséptica*)
4 *botella una jarabe de tos la para* (*una botella de jarabe para la tos*)

What are these medications and what are they for?

2a Mira los dibujos. Con tu compañero/a, haz una conversación entre el/la farmacéutico/a y el/la cliente. (AT2/3–4) [9L6]

✉ *Speaking and interacting with others, Level D*

Speaking. Working in pairs, pupils take it in turns to ask the pharmacist for the items in the drawings.

2b Elige un dibujo de **2a** y escribe un diálogo. (AT4/4)

✉ *Writing imaginatively, Level C/D*

Writing. Pupils choose one of the drawings from **2a** and write up the conversation with the pharmacist.

3a Empareja las quejas con los consejos. (AT3/3) [8S3]

✉ *Reading for information/instructions, Level C*

Reading. Pupils match the aches and pains (1–5) with the advice (a–e).

Answers

1 d	**2** c	**3** a	**4** e	**5** b

3b Escucha y comprueba tus respuestas. [8S3]

✉ *Listening for information/instructions, Level B*

Listening. Pupils listen to the recording and correct their answers to **3a**.

Tapescript

1 – Tengo dolor de muelas.
– Debes ir al dentista.
2 – Tengo tos.
– Debes tomar este jarabe.
3 – Tengo dolor de cabeza.
– Debes tomar unas aspirinas.
4 – Tengo una insolación.
– Debes ir a la cama.
5 – Tengo una picadura.
– Debes ponerte una tirita.

3c Mira los dibujos y elige unas quejas. Tu compañero/a da consejos. (AT2/2) [8S3]

✉ *Speaking and interacting with others, Level D*

Speaking. Working in pairs, pupils take it in turns to choose one of the pictures showing different ailments and give advice to treat that particular complaint.

3d Escribe consejos para cada queja en **3c**. (AT3/3) [8S3]

✉ *Exchange information/ideas, Level C*

Writing. Pupils give advice for each complaint in **3c**, starting with *Debes tomar …*

🖱 **ICT activity**

Ask pupils to work with a partner and design a poster using MS Publisher to advertise a particular treatment (for example *una botella de jarabe para la tos*). Make up a brand name (for example 'Tengo tos').

3 En la farmacia

Plenary [8S3]

Get pupils to find out from someone in the class what verb is used in Spanish for 'you should' or 'you ought to' (*debes*).

Quick fire: Give the complaints from **3a** (1–5) and ask pupils to recommend a treatment (without looking in their books). For example: *Tengo tos. Debes tomar este jarabe.* Accept any sensible sounding advice; it doesn't have to be exactly the same as the answers in the book. Or, turn this round and give the treatment – pupils must give you the ailment. For example: *Debes ir al dentista. Tengo dolor de muelas.*

Cuaderno A, page 55

1 Escribe una frase para cada dibujo. (AT3/2)

✖ *Exchange information/ideas, Level B*

Reading. Pupils look at the box and write the words for the items in pictures 1–5.

Answers

> 1 una caja de aspirinas
> 2 una botella de jarabe
> 3 un paquete de tiritas
> 4 un tubo de crema antiséptica
> 5 una caja de pastillas

2a Escribe las palabras en el orden correcto. (AT4/3) [8S1]

✖ *Knowing about language*

Writing. Pupils write the words in the correct order to make sensible sentences.

Answers

> 1 Debes ir al dentista.
> 2 Debes tomar este jarabe.
> 3 Debes ir a la cama.
> 4 Debes ponerte esta crema antiséptica.
> 5 Debes tomar unas aspirinas.

2b Empareja las frases del cuadro con los dibujos apropiados. Luego elige el consejo apropiado de **2a** para cada dibujo. (AT3/3) [8S3]

✖ *Reading for information/ideas, Level B*

Reading. Pupils match the words from the grid with the sentences from activity **2a** for each picture.

Answers

> 1 Tengo tos./Debes tomar este jarabe.
> 2 Tengo una picadura./Debes ponerte esta crema antiséptica.
> 3 Tengo dolor de cabeza./Debes tomar unas aspirinas.
> 4 Tengo dolor de muelas./Debes ir al dentista.
> 5 Tengo gripe./Debes ir a la cama.

4 Hace dos años que estudio español (Pupil's Book pages 98–99)

Main topics

- Talking about how long you have been doing something

Key Framework objectives

- Non-literal meanings 8W8 (Reinforcement)
- Media listening skills 8L2 (Launch)
- Present, past, future 8S7 (Reinforcement)
- Daily life and young people 8C3 (Reinforcement)
- Sequencing 8S1 (Reinforcement)

Grammar

- *Hace ... que*

Key language

¿Cuánto tiempo hace que ...?
juegas al fútbol/al voleibol/al hockey/al tenis
practicas la equitación/la gimnasia/el judo
vives en Londres
estudias francés

Hace ... un mes	*dos años*
dos meses	*cinco años*
un año	*diez años*

que juego al baloncesto/al rugby/al golf.
que practico la equitación/el ciclismo.
que vivo en Escocia.
que estudio español.

Resources

Cassette C, side 1
CD 3, tracks 25 and 26
Cuaderno A, page 56

Starter 1 [8W5]

Aim: Revising idioms that take *hacer.*

Ask pupils to write down as many phrases as they can think of that take *hacer.* You could give a bit more direction and draw some weather symbols on the board. Or act out: Phew, it's hot, Brrrr, it's cold, etc.

Suggestion

Introduce the structure *Hace ... que ...* Bring in some photos or pictures (taken from magazines, etc.) of 'things that you do'. For example: *Hace veinte años que hablo español, hace un mes que juego al baloncesto, hace cinco años que vivo en ... ,* etc.

Alternatively, ask a language assistant, or student teacher to talk about some of the things they do/study.

1 Elige la frase apropiada para cada dibujo. (AT3/3) [8W8; 8S7]

✖ *Reading for information/instructions, Level C*

Reading. Pupils choose the appropriate phrase to go with each drawing.

Answers

1 d	2 a	3 e	4 b	5 c

2 Escucha y escribe cuánto tiempo hace que cada persona practica su deporte. (1–5) (AT1/2) [8L3]

✖ *Listening for information/instructions, Level C*

Listening. Pupils listen to the recording and write down how long each person has been practising their sport.

Answers

1 10 años	**2** 7 años	**3** 5 años	**4** 1 año	**5** 2 años

Tapescript

1 – ¿Cuánto tiempo hace que juegas al fútbol?
– Hace diez años.
2 – ¿Cuánto tiempo hace que practicas el atletismo?
– Hace siete años.
3 – ¿Cuánto tiempo hace que practicas el ciclismo?
– Hace cinco años.
4 – ¿Hace mucho tiempo que juegas al golf?
– No, hace sólo un año que juego.
5 – ¿Cuánto tiempo hace que practicas el surfing?
– Hace dos años ... y me encanta.

3a Con tu compañero/a, pregunta y contesta. (AT2/3) [8S1, 7]

✖ *Speaking and interacting with others, Level D/E*

Speaking. Working in pairs, pupils take it in turns to ask each other how long they have been doing various things.

➕ Introduce a question to find out what sports they practise, languages they study, etc. Then find out how long they have been doing them. For example: *¿Qué deportes practicas? Practico fútbol. ¿Cuánto tiempo hace que practicas el fútbol? Hace 2 años que practico el fútbol.* [8L5]

4 Hace dos años que estudio español

Aim: Revise 1st, 2nd, 3rd person singular of *jugar, practicar, vivir, estudiar.*

Ask pupils to write down the Spanish for the following:

I play, you play, he plays/I practise, you practise, she practises/I live, you live, he lives/I study, you study, she studies (Mix these up if you feel your class is confident at conjugating verbs).

3b Escribe una frase para cada dibujo. (AT4/3) [8S7]

✕ *Exchange information/ideas, Level C/D*

Writing. Pupils write a sentence for each drawing.

Answers

Hace tres años que Alba estudia inglés.
Hace un año que Rubén vive en Madrid.
Hace cinco años que Marta practica el judo.
Hace seis años que Javi juega al baloncesto.
Hace tres meses que Irene vive en Londres.

3c Escribe cinco frases sobre ti empleando las palabras apropiadas del cuadro de **3a**. (AT4/4) [8S1, 7]

✕ *Exchange information/ideas, Level C/D*

Writing. Pupils write down five sentences about themselves, how long they have been doing something, living somewhere, etc., using the words in the writing frame on page 98 to help them.

🖙 **ICT activity**

Ask pupils to word process this description and make alterations, if necessary, after it has been corrected.

4a Lee y escucha. [8L2; 8C3]

✕ *Knowing about language*

Reading/Listening. Pupils follow and listen to the interview with Sergio on page 99.

Tapescript

– ¡Hola! ¿Cómo te llamas?
– Me llamo Sergio.
– ¿Cuánto tiempo hace que patinas?
– Hace tres años.
– ¿Cómo aprendes la técnica?
– Aprendes en la calle, con los amigos.
– ¿Qué llevas para patinar?
– Llevo ropa cómoda: pantalones anchos, una camiseta y zapatillas.
– ¿Cuántas horas a la semana patinas?

– ¡Muchas! Sobre todo los fines de semana cuando tengo más tiempo libre.

4b Contesta a las preguntas sobre la entrevista en **4a**. (AT3/5) [8C3]

✕ *Reading for information/instructions, Level E*

Reading. Pupils answer questions 1–4 in English.

Answers

1 3 years   **2** in the street   **3** comfortable clothing: wide trousers, t-shirt and trainers   **4** weekends

🖙 **ICT activity**

'Newsletter' format. Pupils conduct an interview with a partner based on Sergio's interview. You could also record it on recording.

En casa

Personal Dossier. Ask pupils to write down four things about themselves (a sport they practise, an instrument they play, a language they speak, the village/town where they live) and say how long they have been practising, playing, studying it, or living there.

Ask pupils to give you two strategies they use to help them understand and answer questions. Take feedback.

Cuaderno A, page 56

1 Lee los datos. ¿Quién dice cada frase? Escribe A, B o C. (AT3/4)

✕ *Reading for information/instructions, Level D*

Reading. Pupils look at the three ID cards and write down the initial of the person they think best suits the description next to each speech bubble, 1–6.

Answers

1 B   **2** A   **3** B   **4** C   **5** A   **6** C

2 Escribe frases sobre ti. (AT4/4) [8S6]

✕ *Exchange information/ideas, Level C/D*

Writing. Using 'hace': Pupils write sentences about themselves.

5 No hay que comer chocolate todos los días (Pupil's Books pages 100–101)

Main topics

- Talking about a healthy lifestyle
- Saying what you should, shouldn't do

Key Framework objectives

- Connectives in extended sentences 8S2
- Modal verbs 8S3 (Reinforcement)
- Media listening skills 8L2 (Reinforcement)
- Present, past, *future* 8S7 (Reinforcement)

Grammar

- *(No) Hay que* + verb
- *(No) Tienes que* + verb
- Immediate future: *voy a* + infinitive

Key language

(No) Hay que beber 2 litros de agua al día.
(No) Tienes que hacer deporte tres veces a la semana.

Resources

Cassette C, side 2
CD 3, tracks 27 and 28
Cuaderno A, page 57
Starters 1 and 2, Resource and Assessment File, page 112

Starter 1

Aim: Revising and categorising infinitives/glossary work.

Using *Resource and Assessment File*, page 112, ask pupils to write the following infinitives under the appropriate group (*-ar, -er, -ir*), and give their meanings. Three of the infinitives are irregular, which ones are they?

Verbs: *comer, beber, hacer, practicar, dormir, descansar, jugar, ir, salir, nadar, correr* (add more or delete some of these depending on your class).

1a Empareja las frases (1–5) con los dibujos apropiados. (AT3/3) [8S3]

✂ *Reading for information/instructions, Level D*

Reading. Pupils match the sentences with the appropriate drawings.

Answers

1 b	**2** c	**3** a	**4** e	**5** d

1b Escucha y comprueba tus respuestas.

✂ *Listening for information/instructions, Level B*

Listening. Pupils listen to the recording and correct their answers.

Tapescript

a *Hay que comer 5 raciones de fruta o verdura al día.*
b *Hay que beber 2 litros de agua al día.*
c *Tienes que hacer deporte tres veces a la semana.*
d *Tienes que desayunar todos los días.*
e *Hay que comer tres comidas al día.*

1c Elige frases de **1a**. Tu compañero/a indica los dibujos apropiados. (AT2/3) [8S1, 3]

✂ *Speaking to convey information, Level B*

Speaking. Working in pairs, one pupil chooses sentences from **1a** and their partner tells them which drawing they correspond to.

2 Escribe cinco frases para dar tus opiniones sobre cómo vivir sano. (AT4/4) [8S1, 3]

✂ *Exchange information/ideas, Level C/D*

Writing. Pupils write five sentences about how to live healthily.

➕ Ask pupils to write four things you shouldn't do if you want to live healthily.

🗩 ICT activity

Ask pupils to design a poster using MS Publisher (or an equivalent) to encourage other pupils in their school to live healthily. Have a competition to choose the best one.

Suggestion

This is such an important cross-curricular topic perhaps you could get together with other departments such as technology, geography, IT, drama, sports and come up with a project you could all carry out together. You could have a school 'get healthy campaign'.

5 No hay que comer chocolate todos los días

Aim: To revise more infinitives.

Write the following on the board, or prepare an OHT using *Resource and Assessment File*, page 112. Ask pupils to fill in the gaps. You may wish to write the infinitives down somewhere on the board for pupils to choose from.

1 (*beber*) *Hay que … 2 litros de agua al día.*
2 (*hacer*) *Tienes que … deporte.*
3 (*comer*) *Hay que … tres comidas al día.*
4 (*desayunar*) *Tienes que … todos los días.*

3 Escucha. Copia y completa las frases. (AT1/3) [8L2]

✉ *Listening for information/instructions, Level D*

Listening/Reading. Pupils listen to the recording and fill in the gaps to Lucía and Gerardo's conversation.

Answers

| 1 deporte | 2 desayunar | 3 fruta | 4 patatas fritas |
| 5 agua | 6 nadar | | |

Tapescript

– *¿Qué vas a hacer para tener una vida más sana, Lucía?*
– *Voy a hacer deporte todos los días.*
– *¿Y tú, Gerardo?*
– *Voy a desayunar.*
– *¿Todos los días?*
– *Sí, todos los días. También voy a comer más fruta y verduras. No voy a comer patatas fritas.*
– *Yo, voy a beber más agua y voy a nadar.*

4a Lee y contesta a las preguntas. (AT3/5)

✉ *Reading for information/instructions, Level E*

Reading. Ask pupils to look at the speech bubbles at the bottom of page 101 and answer 1–5 by writing the initial of the person it refers to.

Answers

| 1 R | 2 L | 3 M | 4 L | 5 C |

4b Escribe sobre lo que vas a hacer durante el verano. (AT4/5) [8S2, 7; 8T5]

✉ *Exchange information/ideas, Level C/E*

Writing. Pupils use the immediate future to write about what they are going to do in the summer.

🔊 **ICT activity**

Ask pupils to word process this and illustrate.

Ask pupils to tell you what words you would use to form the immediate future (*voy a* + infinitive). What is the immediate future? What is an infinitive? Ask pupils to each think of an example of something they are going to do.

Cuaderno A, page 57

1a Escribe las palabras apropiadas en los espacios para dar tus opiniones sobre la vida sana. (AT3/4) [8S3]

✉ *Reading for information/instructions, Level D*

Reading. Pupils fill in the gaps for 1–10 with *(no) hay que/(no) tienes que* to give their opinion about healthy eating.

1b Completa las frases con las ideas de **1a** para expresar tus propias opiniones. (AT3/4; AT4/3) [8S3]

✉ *Exchange information/ideas, Level C*

Writing/Reading. Pupils complete sentences 1–3 with ideas from activity **1a** to express their own opinions.

2 Escribe frases para decir lo que vas o no vas a hacer para estar en forma. (AT4/5) [8S7]

✉ *Exchange information/ideas, Level C/E*

Writing. Using '*voy a*' or '*no voy a*', pupils write sentences to say what they are going do to be fit.

Resumen

This is a checklist of language covered in Module 6. There is a comprehensive *Resumen* list for Module 6 in the Pupil's Book (page 102) and a *Resumen* test sheet in Cuaderno A (page 62).

Prepárate

A revision test to give practice for the test itself at the end of the module.

Resources

Cassette C, side 2
CD 3, tracks 29, 30 and 31
Cuaderno A, pages 58, 59, 60, 61 and 62
Resumen, Resource and Assessment File, page 120
Skills, Resource and Assessment File, pages 118 and 119

---

1 Escucha y escribe la letra apropiada para cada parte del cuerpo. (1–10) (AT1/2) [8L3]

✉ *Listening for information/instructions, Level B*

Listening. Pupils listen to the recording and write down the letters of the parts of the body in the correct order. NB *No 8: la rodilla is not shown on the picture.*

Answers

1 a	**2** e	**3** b	**4** d	**5** j	**6** f	**7** g	**8** f	**9** h	**10** c

Tapescript

1 *Me duele la cabeza.*
2 *¿Te duele el brazo?*
3 *Me duele la garganta.*
4 *¿Qué te duele?*
  Me duele la espalda.
5 *Me duelen las muelas.*
6 *Me duele la mano.*
7 *Me duele la pierna.*
8 *¿Qué te duele?*
  Me duele la rodilla.
9 *Me duelen los pies.*
10 *¡Ay! Me duele mucho el estómago.*

2a Escucha y elige el dibujo apropiado. (1–4) (AT1/3) [8L3]

✉ *Listening for information/instructions, Level D*

Listening. Pupils listen to the recording and choose the appropriate drawing.

Answers

1 c	**2** b	**3** a	**4** d

Tapescript

1 – *¿Tiene algo para la tos?*
  – *Para la tos, le recomiendo este jarabe.*
  – *Bueno, deme una botella grande, por favor.*
2 – *Me duele mucho la cabeza.*
  – *Bueno, puede tomar aspirinas.*
  – *Vale. Deme una caja de aspirinas, por favor. Una caja pequeña.*
3 – *Hola. ¿Cómo puedo ayudarle?*

  – *Tengo unas picaduras. ¿Qué recomienda usted para las picaduras?*
  – *A ver ... esta crema es buena.*
  – *Deme un tubo pequeño, por favor.*
4 – *¿Tiene algo para la diarrea?*
  – *Para la diarrea recomiendo estas pastillas.*
  – *Deme una caja por favor, ¡una caja grande!*

2b Escucha otra vez y elige el dibujo de la medicina apropiada. (AT1/3) [8L3]

✉ *Listening for information/instructions, Level D*

Listening. Pupils listen to the recording again and write down the letter of the appropriate medicine.

Answers

1 f cough syrup/large	**2 i** aspirin/small
3 l cream/small	**4 g** tablets/large

Tapescript

As for activity **2a**

---

3 Mira los dibujos en **2a** otra vez y di a tu compañero/a lo que te pasa. (AT2/2)

✉ *Speaking to convey information, Level C*

Speaking. Working in pairs, pupils take it in turns to choose four of the drawings from **2a** and say what is wrong with them.

---

4 Empareja las quejas con los consejos. (AT3/3) [8S3]

✉ *Reading for information/instructions, Level C*

Reading. Pupils match the ailments with the advice.

Answers

1 d	**2** c	**3** a	**4** b

---

5 ¿Qué te pasa? Describe los dibujos. (AT4/2–4)

✉ *Exchange information/ideas, Level B/D*

Writing. Pupils write sentences describing the ailments in the drawings.

Cuaderno A, page 58

Repaso

1a Completa el diálogo en la farmacia. (AT3/4) [9L6]

✉ *Reading for information/instructions, Level D*

Reading. Pupils choose suitable words from the box to fill in the gaps to the conversation in the chemist's.

Answers

> 1 garganta 2 pastillas 3 tos 4 botella 5 cabeza
> 6 fiebre 7 aspirinas

1b Marca los síntomas que tiene el chico. (AT3/3)

✉ *Reading for information/instructions, Level D*

Reading. Pupils tick the boxes to show what the boy's symptoms in activity **1a** are.

Answers

> Le duele la cabeza. Tiene dolor de garganta.
> Tiene fiebre. Tiene tos.

Cuaderno A, page 59

Repaso (*contd.*)

1c Marca la medicina y los consejos del farmaceútico. (AT3/3) [9L6]

✉ *Reading for information/instructions, Level D*

Reading. Pupils tick the medicine and advice given by the pharmacist.

Answers

> aspirina (4 veces al día), jarabe para el tos, pastillas para
> el dolor de garganta

2 Escribe diálogos en la farmacia. (AT3/3)

✉ *Reading for information/instructions, Level C*

Reading. Pupils look at the three pictures and choose two appropriate speech bubbles to go with each picture.

Answers

> 1 Tengo dolor de estómago y diarrea. Estas pastillas son
>   buenas.
> 2 ¿Tiene algo para las picaduras? Esta pomada es muy
>   buena.
> 3 ¿Tiene algo para la insolación? Esta crema es muy
>   buena.

Cuaderno A, page 60

Gramática 1

1 Complete the sentences with *el, la, los* or *las.*

✉ *Knowing about language*

Answers

> 1 la 2 los 3 la 4 el 5 las 6 la 7 el 8 las 9 la

2 Complete the sentences with *duele* or *duelen.*

✉ *Knowing about language*

Answers

> 1 duele 2 duele 3 duele 4 duele 5 duele 6 duelen

3 Choose words from the grid to write sentences about yourself.

✉ *Knowing about language*

Answers (*example*)

> Visito a mis abuelos una vez a la semana.

Cuaderno A, page 61

Gramática 2

1 Write five sentences using the correct words from the grid.

✉ *Knowing about language*

Answers (*example*)

> Para dormir bien no hay que beber café por la noche.

2 Write sentences using the information in the grid.

✉ *Knowing about language*

Pupils use the words '*hace ... que ...*' to help them write their sentences.

Skills, Resource and Assessment File, page 118 (Word games)

1

Answers

> **a** 27 (all parts of the body except *train*)
> **b** 23 (all illnesses except *year*)
> **c** 25 (all containers except *water*)
> **d** 18 (all parts of the body except *§ eat*)
> **e** 22 (all dates/lengths of time except *breakfast*)
> **f** 28 (all nationalities except *leg*)
> **g** 3 (all illnesses except *aspirin*)
> **h** 26 (all types of transport except *packet*)

2

Answers

> **a** pequeño
> **b** una lechuga
> **c** los dedos
> **d** una farmacia
> **e** el jarabe
> **f** España
> **g** el desayuno
> **h** un plátano
> **i** el agua
> **j** el ciclismo

3

Answers

> **a** cabeza
> **b** jarabe
> **c** aspirinas
> **d** oídos
> **e** tos
> **f** estómago
>
> Sentence a, c and e lead you to the winning line.
> c, d, f would also give you a winning line.
>
> Pupils add sentences of their own to give another winning line.

Skills, Resource and Assessment File, page 119 (Connectives)

1

Answers

para terminar	finally
también	also
y	*and*
pero	but
porque	because
siempre	always
por eso	so

2

Answers

> Doctor Muñoz
> No sé que me pasa. Estoy cansado **porque** no puedo dormir. **Siempre** estoy sin energía **por eso** es difícil hacer mis deberes. **También** tengo dolor de cabeza. Tengo hambre pero no puedo comer. **Para terminar** estoy nervioso **y** trabajo demasiado. ¿Qué me aconsejas?
> Ana

3

Answers

así que	so
cuando	when
o	or
si	if

4

Pupils make use of the connectives they have practised to write their own letter about how to keep healthy using the prompts given.

6 ¡Extra! Entrevista con una deportista. (Pupil's Book pages 104–105)

Main topics

This is an optional extension unit which revises and extends some of the key language of the module: it features an interview with a cyclist talking about how long she has been in her chosen career and what she hopes to do in the future.

Key Framework objectives

- Present, past, future 8S7 (Reinforcement)
- Using high frequency words 8S8 (Reinforcement)
- Language and text types 8T3 (Reinforcement)
- Media listening skills 8L2 (Reinforcement)

Grammar

- *Hace ... que ...*
- *Voy a* + infinitive

Resources

Cassette C, side 2
CD 3, tracks 32 and 33

Starter 1 [8S7]

Aim: To revise the immediate future.

Brainstorm. Find out as many things as you can about what pupils would like to do in the future and write these on the board under the heading *Voy a ...*

1a Lee y escucha la entrevista. [8S7; 8T3; 8L3]

✖ *Reading for information/instructions, Level E*

Reading/Listening. Ask pupils to listen to the recording and follow the interview with Joane Somarriba.

Tapescript

- ¡Hola, Joane! ¿Cuánto tiempo hace que practicas el ciclismo?
- ¡Hace veinte años!
- ¿Cómo es la vida de una ciclista profesional?
- Tienes que entrenar muchas horas y todos los días.
- ¿Qué hay que comer?
- Tienes que comer bien. Hay que comer pasta y arroz, también pescado y carne. Y claro, hay que comer fruta y verduras.
- ¿Y de beber?
- Tienes que beber mucha agua.
- ¿Qué haces en tu tiempo libre?
- ¡Descanso y duermo!
- ¿Qué vas a hacer en el futuro?
- Voy a competir en la primera Vuelta a España femenina. Y espero ganar.

1b Contesta a las preguntas. (AT3/5) [8S8]

✖ *Reading for information/instructions, Level E*

Reading. Ask pupils to answer questions 1–8 in English.

Answers

> **1** cycling **2** Spain **3** Giro de Italia (twice) and Tour de France (once) **4** twenty years **5** every day **6** (healthy) She eats pasta, rice, meat, fish, fruit and vegetables **7** rests and sleeps **8** win the first Vuelta a España

2 Escucha y elige las respuestas apropiadas. (AT1/4) [8S7; 8L3]

✖ *Listening for information/instructions, Level E*

Listening. Pupils listen to the recording and do the multiple choice for 1–5.

Answers

> **1** c **2** b **3** a **4** b **5** a

Tapescript

1 – ¡Hola! ¿Cómo te llamas?
– Me llamo Óscar Sevilla.
– ¿De dónde eres?
– Soy de España. Soy español.
2 – ¿Cuánto tiempo hace que practicas el ciclismo?
– Hace quince años.
3 – ¿En qué carreras competiste este año?
– En el Tour de Francia, en el Giro de Italia y también en la Vuelta a España.
4 – ¿Qué vas a hacer en el futuro?
– Voy a entrenar más.
5 – ¿Vas a entrenar más?
– Sí, sí y espero ganar el Tour de Francia.

3 ¿Qué vas a hacer en el futuro? Emplea frases del cuadro y habla con tu compañero/a. (AT2/5) [8S7]

✖ *Experiences, feelings, opinions, Level D/E*

Speaking. Working in pairs, pupils use sentences from the vocabulary frame at the bottom of page 105 to help them talk about what they want to do in the future.

módulo 6

4 Escribe un párrafo para decir lo que vas y no vas a hacer en el futuro. (AT4/5) [8S5, 7; 8T5]

Exchange information/ideas, Level D/E

Writing. Pupils write down five sentences to describe what they are going to do in the future and what they are not going to do.

Plenary

Ask pupils to work with a partner and write down two strategies they use to help them tackle large pieces of text such as the interview with Joane Somarriba. Take feedback.

● Self-access reading and writing at two levels.

A Reinforcement

1 Empareja las frases con los dibujos. (AT3/2)

✉ *Reading for information/instructions, Level B*

Reading. Pupils match the sentences with the drawings.

Answers

1 f	2 g	3 h	4 d	5 e	6 b	7 a	8 c

2 Empareja las dos partes correctas de cada frase para los dibujos a–e. (AT3/3) [8S1]

✉ *Reading for information/instructions, Level C*

Reading. Pupils match the two sentence halves to make a full sentence for drawings a–e.

Answers

1 Hace cinco años que juego al fútbol.
2 Hace tres años que toco la guitarra.
3 Hace diez años que vivo en Madrid.
4 Hace dos años que estudio español.
5 Hace cuatro años que practico la gimnasia.

3 Escribe frases para ti. (AT4/4) [8S1]

✉ *Exchange information/ideas, Level C*

Writing. Ask pupils to write sentences about themselves using a similar format to the answers in 2.

B Extension

1 Empareja las frases con los dibujos. (AT3/2)

✉ *Reading for information/instructions, Level B*

Reading. Pupils match the sentences with the drawings.

Answers

1 e	2 f	3 a	4 b	5 d	6 c

2 Empareja los textos a–d con los textos 1–4. (AT3/5) [8S7]

✉ *Reading for information/instructions, Level D*

Reading. Pupils match texts a–d with texts 1–4.

Answers

a 4	b 2	c 1	d 3

3 Tus amigos están enfermos en España pero no hablan español. Escríbeles unas frases para decir al médico. (AT4/3–5)

✉ *Exchange information/ideas, Level C/D*

Writing. Pupils look at the pictures and write down sentences for friends who have taken ill in Spain and don't speak any Spanish so that they can explain what is wrong with them to the doctor.